CHIPPY'S GOLF BOOK

A *Right* Handed Step By Step Reference Guide

(How To Improve Your Swing Fundamentals & Game Strategy)

DAVID CHAPMAN

Order this book online at www.trafford.com
or email orders@trafford.com

Most Trafford titles are also available at major online book retailers.

Print information available on the last page.

ISBN: 978-1-4907-7796-2 (sc)
ISBN: 978-1-4907-7797-9 (e)

Trafford rev.   10/19/2016

 www.trafford.com
North America & international
toll-free: 1 888 232 4444 (USA & Canada)
fax: 812 355 4082

Table Of Contents

E. Putting Course Management

F. Swinging Thought Processes

G. Managing Your Game

H. Bibliography

(A)
Fullswing

(A-1) The Grip

Key Points

- This is the main fundamental golf grip used for all golf clubs except the putter.
- Gripping a golf club is totally different and much more delicate than gripping a baseball bat.
- You need to hold the club handle more in your fingers than in your palm for a golf grip. It will feel like you are holding a yardstick, not like you are holding a baseball bat. Don't let the club handle slide back into your palm. Keep the club handle up in your fingers or you will lose the feel, delicacy, touch, smoothness, rhythm & accuracy of your swing.
- You need the grip on your golf club to be precise & correct or it will cause your golf swing to go wrong. An incorrect grip will cause a chain reaction of incorrect sequences that will ruin your golf swing by the time it gets to the hitting zone.
- Making a correct golf grip is similar to sighting a gun. The front site and back site is what you line up on a gun. Making sure that your hands are in the correct position with a square clubface directly at your target are what you line up to site a golf grip.
- Just because your golf grip feels comfortable doesn't necessarily make it correct. But, feeling comfortable, being relaxed and having a natural smooth finger feeling swing is very important too.

Both Hands Become One

- It's very important to have both your hands as snug together as possible so that they are able to work together and feel as one distinct unit. You don't want to have your hands fighting against each other throughout the swing.
- It's much easier to keep together an accurate, smooth & rhythmic swing when both of your hands are melded together as one.
- Your left hand is a control hand which helps to keep the clubface square throughout the entire swing and your right hand is simply a following hand which also helps to guide the speed through the bottom arc of your swing.
- That said, both of your hands still need to feel as one hand, not two hands throughout the entire swing.

Light Grip Pressure

- Never grip a golf club tightly. You need to grip each club as lightly as you can. Grip each club just light enough so that you have control & feel over it. Don't grip a golf club so tightly that you are wrist locked.
- Every club's grip pressure will be slightly different. The driver will be your tightest grip and your grip pressure will get progressively lighter and lighter all the way down to the wedges which will be the lightest grip pressure of them all. But, even the driver's grip pressure needs to be a fairly light grip.
- The more delicate the swing is, the lighter your grip pressure needs to be. The more aggressive the swing is, the tighter your grip pressure needs to be.
- A light grip will also help to make sure your clubface goes through impact in the square position.
- Make sure your right hand grips the club handle as equally tight as your left hand.

Steps To Making A Perfect Grip

- Get in your correct address position and place your left hand on the grip.
- Make sure the clubhead is resting on the ground perfectly flat with the clubface perfectly square & lined up directly at your

target. There should still be a little bit of grip visible at the top end of your club handle.

- The club handle runs across your left palm on a slight diagonal from the base of your forefinger to just below the callus under your pinkie finger. Make sure you are holding the club more in your fingers than in your palm.
- Close your fingers around the club handle and place your thumb on top of the grip a touch to the right side pointing straight down towards the clubhead.
- The crease made on your left hand from between your thumb and forefinger should be pointing to just outside your right ear. You will see approximately 2 ½ knuckles on this hand.
- Your left hand and forearm should both be square to the target pointing in the exact same direction as the square clubface.
- Place your right hand on the grip making sure it is square to the clubface as well.
- Your right hand needs to hold the grip handle even more in your fingers than your left hand does.
- The club handle runs across your right palm on a slight diagonal crossing through the middle area of your forefinger to the base of your pinkie finger.
- Close your fingers around the club handle and make sure your right forefinger is under the grip in a trigger finger position like it would be on a gun. Place your right thumb on top of the grip just a touch to the left of center pointing straight down towards the clubhead.
- Interlock your left forefinger with your right pinkie finger underneath the grip handle.
- Jam both your hands and interlocking fingers together as closely & snug as you can get them. The grip pressure is still light, but your two hands and interlocking fingers are jammed into each other as tightly as they can to make sure both of your hands feel as one.
- The crease on your right hand made between your thumb and forefinger should be pointing directly at your left shoulder. You will see approximately 2 knuckles on this hand.
- The creases formed by your thumb and forefinger on both of your hands will be forming parallel lines to each other.

3

- Your hands are now in the correct position. You have made the perfect main fundamental golf grip.

(A-2) Address

Club & Ball

- Where you place the ball in your stance is different for every club. Place the ball forward in your stance for long irons and the driver to line up just inside your front left foot. The ball gets positioned progressively back from there more and more for each club until the ball needs to be placed in the very middle of your stance for the short irons & wedges.
- Clubhead is resting on the ground, but barely. It's like resting it on an eggshell. Keep the clubhead up, but make sure it is touching the ground at the same time.
- Clubshaft is exactly 90 degrees perpendicular to your back bone. You will be like a perfectly squared 'L' tilted slightly forwards maintaining the 90-degree clubshaft angle to your backbone.
- Clubface is perfectly square and aimed directly at your target.

Hands

- One closed hand span should be the approximate space that separates your hands out from your thighs.
- Your hands are always forward of the ball for every single swing lined up just over your front left knee. The ball moves progressively back in your stance for higher and higher clubs, but your hands are always positioned forward over your front left knee for every single club you swing. In other words, the higher the club, the more the clubshaft will be tilted forwards towards the target. The lower the club, the less the clubshaft will be tilted forwards towards the target. This is because the ball position changes with each different club, but your hand position doesn't.

4

Arms

- Keep your right elbow tucked in fairly close to the right side of your body.
- Right elbow is loose and under part of elbow is pointing straight down towards the ground, not out and away from you.
- Your right elbow and right arm are free of tension & bend easily at the elbow. Your right arm is very loose and not stiff locked.
- Both of your arms are hanging straight down from your body a touch up from vertical. They are tense free, relaxed & comfortable.
- Let your arms be free & loose from your body.
- Keep your left arm as straight & solid as possible, but don't keep it rigid. Keep it as straight as you can just to the point before you'd lock your elbow.
- Visualize your left arm, left hand & clubshaft as one long rod, one long straight line from your left shoulder all the way down to the clubhead. There is only one hinge on this rod, your left wrist that helps swing the clubshaft back and through on a hinge.
- The tops of your forearms are flexed and caved in towards each other helping you feel more solid & connected.

Shoulders

- Right shoulder is slightly lower than your left shoulder. In other words, your right shoulder is under your left shoulder.
- Right shoulder is not too far back or too far forward, it is lined up directly over your back right knee.
- Both of your shoulders are pushed back and up in the proper posture, but they are not tense. They need to be super loose, comfortable, relaxed and have a smooth lazy feeling.

Head

- Keep your head level to the ground & well behind the ball. Don't tilt your head on an angle.
- Keep your chin up as high as you can. But, make sure you can still easily see the ball down there in front of you.

Back

- Push your butt out slightly, pull your stomach in a little & keep your back as straight as a board.
- The line up your back from your tailbone to the back of your head is as straight as you can possibly make it. There is no curve in your back whatsoever.
- Your lower-back, upper-back & chest all feel upright and very tall.
- Your spine angle is leaning slightly forward so that you have approximately one closed hand span width between your hands on the grip and your thighs.
- Your spine angle is tilted slightly back to the right away from the target.
- Your upper-body and chest are as far behind the ball as they can comfortably get.
- Your hips are tilted forward pointing down towards the ground on a 45 degree angle. In other words, if you are wearing a belt, your belt buckle will be lower than your tailbone.

Legs

- Both legs are slightly bent, flexed & springy so that you feel in control.
- Your legs feel balanced and ready for action. Keep your legs relaxed & tension free so that they are not feeling locked in place. You should be able to feel and use the muscles in the front of your thighs when your knees are bent just enough. It will be easy to rock back and forth on your two feet.
- Knees are perfectly square pointing in front of you. Make sure they are not caved in towards each other.
- Angle your right knee just a touch to the left towards the target.

Feet

- Weight distribution for long irons and the driver are on your back right foot to encourage a more sweeping blow into the ball. 60% of your weight is on your back right foot / 40% of your weight is on your front left foot.

6

- Weight distribution for middle and short irons are even to encourage a more descending blow into the ball. 50% of your weight is on your back right foot / 50% of your weight is on your front left foot.
- 50% of your weight is towards your toes / 50% of your weight is towards your heels is the other weight distribution for all clubs. In other words, always keep your toe & heel weight balanced evenly.
- Feet width will be the widest for long irons & the driver and gets progressively narrower and narrower until narrowest for short irons & wedges. The widest stance you will need to make is for the driver and will be feet just outside shoulder width and as narrow for the wedges as only 6 inches in between the inside of your feet. It all depends on how aggressive or delicate the swing is going to be.

Overall

- Alignment needs to be perfect. Feet, knees, hips, shoulders, forearms, hands, eyes & clubface all run perfectly parallel to your aimline.
- Think of yourself as a tripod with your two feet and clubhead as the three points of contact with the ground. You need to feel like you are gripping the ground.
- You need to be in the ready feeling like a baseball player getting ready to hit a ball or a boxer getting ready to give a great big punching blow. You should feel well planted to the ground, especially your back right leg.
- All of your right side is slightly under the left side of your body.
- You need to feel very tall & upright. Don't become too hunched over.
- Keep everything up & become a solid structure with the correct posture. Keep your head up, back up, legs up, arms up, shoulders up, clubhead up, everything needs to be up, up, up.
- The three components that need to be in the exact same distinct position in your stance for every single swing you make are the ball, hands and feet. Find these correct three positions for each of your different clubs and then always keep them the same. Don't

change the consistently of where you have these components positioned in your stance from swing to swing.

- Don't stand too close to the ball or you'll be too cramped and crunched. Don't stand too far away from the ball or you'll have to overstretch and overreach. Stand just far enough away from the ball where you need to be reaching for it, not too far, but it is definitely a reach. This is because during your swing, your arms will extend slightly out and farther away from your body than they were at address.

Transferring To The Next Stage

- Take a deep breath and then breathe out completely. When you have completely breathed out is the sign, the point in time, the trigger that it is time to start the takeaway.
- Taking a deep breath in and exhaling out will also release all tension and relax your entire body and most importantly your mind.
- Then, continue to breathe normally while you swing, don't continue to hold your breath.

(A-3) Takeaway

Club & Ball

- Start the swing very gently by bringing the clubhead precisely straight back for the first 6 inches of takeaway. A very slow, smooth & steady first movement is always needed.
- All golf swings start out as a sweeping motion, never roll the clubhead away. In other words, don't start hinging your wrists & forearms right away. Don't start by picking the club up or by jerking it away. Always start all your golf swings by pulling the clubhead straight back.
- The first 6 inches straight back is a very rigid and stiff flowing feeling. After this straight back takeaway the swing goes on automatic and flows back and around naturally. But, the first move straight back is essential in order to start everything out on the correct path. Everything else that happens in the swing

is a reaction to this first move, it is a domino effect. Therefore, it is essential to always make sure it is a slow & straight back takeaway for every single swing you make.

- When the clubhead is just past your back right foot, the clubface should be facing a touch right of the ball, not way right and not still looking at the ball.

Arms

- Keep your forearms flexed and caved in towards each other.
- Keep your left arm and clubshaft in a straight line until the momentum of the swinging clubhead causes your wrists to hinge up naturally.

Head

- Don't focus on or watch the clubhead moving away. Always keep your eyes focused on the ball. Your eyes need to be focused on the most specific point you can focus on at the back middle point of the golf ball for the entire swing. The ball is the target of your swing. Don't take your eyes off the target.

Hands

- Keep your hands in as close as you can to your back right leg as you swing back. Don't let your hands swing up and away from you.

Back

- Start each takeaway with your upper-back muscles & shoulders only, not with your arms.

Overall

- Start slow and easy, no jerking, smoothly and gradually picking up speed.

- Your takeaway needs to start effortlessly. Imagine it is like somebody else or some other mysterious force that is taking the clubhead back for you.
- There can't be any tension during this first move of the swing. It must be the most relaxed & smoothest takeaway you can possibly come up with.
- It's a one piece takeaway. Your arms, shoulders, clubhead, clubshaft, hands, elbows, chest, hips and body all need to start away together at the exact same time.
- The swing eventually turns and starts to rotate on a swivel, but the swing never slides backwards at any point.
- Your legs & head need to remain dead still. Don't move either of them even a millimeter as you start moving back in your takeaway.
- Don't start bending your elbows or hinging your wrists until your hands pass over your back right knee.
- Have it set in your mind that you are either getting prepared for a sweeping blow or a descending blow and continue the backswing accordingly.

(A-4) Backswing

Club & Ball

- When your left arm has swung back and is level and exactly horizontal to the ground, the butt-end of your clubshaft should be pointing just in front of your toes for descending type swings and be pointing somewhere in the middle area between your toes and the ball for sweeping type swings.
- Keep the whole backswing in tight. Think of your butt as just touching against a tall flat wall behind you. If the swinging clubhead gets too far behind you, the clubhead will hit the wall. You can never let the clubhead hit the imaginary wall behind you at any point during the backswing.
- Keep the turn in tight and more horizontally for the first half of the swing, then the top half of the backswing is also in tight, but more upwards & vertical.

Hands

- When your left arm has swung back and is level and exactly horizontal to the ground, the back of your right hand should be pointing directly behind you at a 90 degree angle. For sweeping type swings your wrists will only be half hinged up by this point and both thumbs will only be pointing 45 degrees of the way straight up. For descending type swings your wrists will be fully hinged by this point and both thumbs will be pointing straight up 90 degrees to the sky.
- Try your best to keep your hands in synchronization with your swinging body. In other words, keep your hands in front of your chest for the entire backswing.
- Push your hands as far away from your head as possible for the entire backswing. This will encourage the roundest, fullest & smoothest swing possible.

Arms

- Keep the swing in tight & connected. Don't let the swing get loose. Keep both of your arms in close to your body. Don't let them swing out & away from you.
- You don't want your arms so tight that they will feel cramped, but you also don't want your arms getting too far away from your body either.
- Keep your right upper-arm as close to your right side as you can.
- Don't let your arms swing ahead of your upper-body. Your arms and body are synchronized so that both parts stay connected for the entire backswing. Your arms need to remain in front of your body, don't let your arms get too far ahead and don't let them get too far behind for the entire backswing. Let your arms flow with the natural turning motion of your upper-body.
- Keep your right elbow comfortable & as close to your right side as you can. It's almost like your right elbow is attached to your right hip for the entire backswing. Only let your right elbow get away you from your right hip at the top half of the backswing when everything goes upwards. Other than that, keep your right elbow in as close as you can to your right hip.
- Keep your forearms caved in towards each other for as long as you can in the backswing.

11

- Keep your elbows as close as they can to each other for the entire backswing. The distance between your elbows always stays the same, even at the top part of the backswing. Don't let your elbows break apart from each other.
- Don't jerk or lift your arms up in the backswing. Let your arms flow back naturally at the same speed as your turning shoulders.

Shoulders

- Both of your shoulders turn back, but only concentrate & think about your left shoulder. Turn your left shoulder smoothly, constantly, consistently and deliberately as far back as you can without forcing it. Stretch it back to the point where you know it is 100% fully coiled & in the slot under your chin.

Head

- Your head cannot move or bounce up or down during the backswing, not even a millimeter.
- Your head stays perfectly level to the ground & stays at the exact same height for the entire backswing.
- Your head can eventually slide slightly back towards your back right knee if necessary for the more aggressive swings, but your head can never move up or down.
- Keep your chin up high for the entire backswing.

Back

- Turn your back to the target. Make sure you turn all the way away from the ball. In other words, a full 90 degree turn. Don't get lazy and just lift your arms and hands to get the club back there, turn your whole upper-body.
- Spine angle stays leaning forward at the same angle it was at address and stays at that exact same angle throughout the entire backswing.
- Spine angle stays tilted back to the right and away from the target for the entire backswing.
- Turn your hips until they are flexed tight, until they stop turning which will be at a 45 degree turn. Your hips cannot turn a full

90 degrees to the target & your hips will be fully turned by the halfway point in your backswing.

Legs

- Don't twist your legs in the backswing. Keep & maintain a stable base.
- Your back right knee maintains its flex the same as it was at address and is quite sturdy and braced. This makes it impossible for your hips to turn past 45 degrees & will allow your upper-body and shoulders to coil up tightly.
- Your front left knee doesn't need to be as flexed as your back right knee, but it still needs to have some flex in it.

Feet

- All of the weight of your body is moving back towards your back right foot.
- When shifting your weight, keep it in control. You don't want to shift your weight too fast or get too sloppy and jerky with it. Flow with it slowly and smoothly at your own natural tempo and rhythm.
- Keep your front left heel grounded throughout the entire backswing.

Overall

- The first part of the backswing is more horizontal and the second half of the backswing is more vertical.
- Swing the clubhead back until your left arm is level & horizontal to the ground and then it is more of an upwards motion after that.
- Turn as far as you can go back on a swivel until your lower-body becomes so flexed it can no longer turn. Then, your upper-body continues to turn more upwards & vertical to the very top of the backswing.
- Your upper-body coils up tightly against your lower-body.
- The final part in the backswing is when your hands, arms & elbows comfortably flex against your chest and form the perfect

box structure which is the position you want to be in at the very top of a fullswing backswing.

- Make sure you are winding up in the correct sequence. In the backswing, you wind up from the top down the opposite way that you unwind in the downswing. As you approach the very top of the backswing top parts finish first and bottom parts finish last. Firstly, the clubhead stops. Secondly, your arms stop. Thirdly, your shoulders & upper-body stop. Lastly, your knees, legs and feet stop. (Note: Your hips are the only part that stop halfway through the backswing because they only need to coil 45 degrees)

Transferring To The Next Stage

- You will now be standing very tall & erect with your hands up high in the perfect box structure at the very top of the backswing.
- You are fully wound up like a coil.

(A-5) Top Of Backswing

Club & Ball

- The clubshaft will be just above your head perfectly level & horizontal to the ground & pointing on a line parallel to your aimline towards the target. The clubshaft needs to get to horizontal & be perfectly level to the ground for a fullswing backswing, but don't ever let the clubshaft go past horizontal.
- Think of your butt as just touching against a tall flat wall behind you and your clubhead is just out in front of that wall. Your clubhead is not allowed to be touching the imaginary wall behind you.
- Make sure the clubface is still perfectly square in your hands. In other words, the clubface angle will still be the exact same as your left forearm and will be pointing at approximately a 45 degree angle between the ground and the sky when you are at the very top part of the backswing in the perfect box structure. If the clubface is open, it will be pointing directly towards the ground.

If the clubface is closed, it will be pointing directly towards the sky.

Hands

- Both of your wrists are fully hinged and form a 90 degree angle to your right forearm.
- Make sure your grip pressure hasn't changed and is the exact same light grip pressure it was at address. Consciously think about your hands and know that they have not loosened or tightened at all, especially your left control hand.
- Push your hands up in the air as high as you can push them.

Arms

- The under part of your right upper-arm is level & horizontal to the ground.
- Your left arm is not perfectly straight, but is straightened and stretched out as straight as you can make it forming a diagonal line from under your chin out to your hands.
- You left arm is firm, but comfortable & relaxed with some softness to it. There is a slight bend in your left elbow to help keep the top of your backswing tension free.
- Both of your arms are fairly firm in order to hold the perfect box structure together & in place. But, don't let your muscles tighten too much. Your arms still need to be comfortable & soft, tension free, relaxed & be ready for the free flowing swing downwards.
- Never try to control your arms, not even at the very top of the backswing, let them flow into the perfect box structure & flow out of the perfect box structure naturally & effortlessly.

Shoulders

- Your front left shoulder needs to be fully turned 90 degrees and is now in the slot nice and tight under your chin.
- Your front left shoulder is now well behind the ball.
- Both of your shoulders are fully turned. In other words, they have both made a full 90 degree turn from their address position.

Head

- Your head is in the same position as it was at address, it hasn't moved back, up or down at all, not even a millimeter. (Note: For more aggressive swings your head may of slid back a bit, but never up or down)
- Your head is still level and is at the exact same height as it was at address.
- Keep your chin held up high.

Back

- Your back has fully turned 90 degrees and your back is now facing the target.
- Your hips have fully turned at a 45 degree turn.

Legs

- Both legs are braced and balanced getting ready for the downswing. Like a boxer getting ready to give a great big punching blow.
- Your back right knee has some extra flex in it as most of the weight is now on your back right leg.
- You are coiled up tightly into your back right leg.

Feet

- Your front left heel is still on the ground. Don't lift it up. The whole sole of your front left foot is still flat on the ground.
- Almost all of your weight will now be on your back right foot. But, don't let the weight move all the way to the outside of your back right foot. Keep the weight shifting back in control and balanced.

Overall

- Consciously & deliberately pause for a split second. Take a split second to allow everything to catch up before you change direction to the downswing.

- There can't be any strain in the perfect box structure at the top of your backswing. It needs to be very relaxed & comfortable without any tension.
- Your body will be coiled up so tight that it can't coil up any farther. This is where all the power comes from that will be transferred into the downswing.
- The tighter you wind up in the backswing, the faster you will unwind in the downswing and the more powerful your swing will be.

The Perfect Box Structure

- Your swinging arms & club will now be up in the perfect box structure just above and behind your head.
- Your right upper-arm, right forearm and clubshaft will form a square box structure with all corners at exactly 90 degree angles.
- Both of your wrists & both thumbs are fully hinged to form a 90 degree angle to your right forearm.
- Both of your thumbs are level & horizontal to the ground pointing on a parallel line to your aimline towards the target.
- Clubshaft is level & horizontal to the ground pointing on a parallel line to your aimline towards the target.
- Clubshaft forms a 90 degree angle to your right forearm.
- Right forearm is at a 90 degree angle to your right upper-arm.
- Right upper-arm is level & horizontal to the ground parallel to the clubshaft.
- Your left arm is stretched out on a diagonal across your chest connected to this perfect box structure.

Transferring To The Next Stage

- Don't rush into the downswing so jerkily or quickly. A super smooth transition is needed. The transfer to the downswing is an almost lazy feeling.
- If you don't take a split second to let everything catch up in the backswing, your downswing will break down in the transfer.

(A-6) Downswing

Club & Ball

- You will literally feel the clubhead lag behind for a split second at the very start of the downswing.
- Wait for the clubhead to drop down, don't force the clubhead down. Make sure the clubhead starts off on the correct path by not rushing into it, but by transferring the direction from backswing to downswing slowly & purposely.
- The clubhead lags behind so much at the top of the backswing that it will need to be catching up for the entire downswing. The clubhead won't fully catch up until the moment of impact at the bottom arc of your swing.
- When your left arm is halfway back down in the downswing, when it is level & horizontal with the ground again, the butt-end of your clubshaft should be pointing more towards the ball for descending type swings and just outside the ball for sweeping type swings. (Note: This is farther out then the butt-end of your clubshaft was pointing in the backswing)
- Keep the whole downswing in tight. Think of your butt as just touching against a tall flat wall behind you. If the swinging clubhead swings out too far behind you on the way down, the clubhead will hit the wall. You can never let the clubhead hit the imaginary wall behind you at any point during the downswing.

Hands

- Don't suddenly tighten or jerk your hands when you start the downswing. Remember to maintain the exact same grip pressure throughout the entire swing.
- Keep your wrists fully hinged for the entire start of the downswing. Don't start unhinging your wrists until your hands are just above hip height.
- Concentrate on feeling your hands and always keep your hands in as close to your body as you can. Don't let your hands fling out and away from you.
- You need to keep your hands directly out and in front of your chest as soon as you start the downswing and keep them there

18

throughout the entire downswing. Don't let your hands fall behind.

Arms

- Keep your left forearm and clubshaft at a 90 degree angle until your left arm is level & horizontal to the ground again. At this point, your wrists begin to unhinge quickly & aggressively getting ready to thwack through the hitting zone.
- Keep your elbows squeezed in tight towards each other for the entire downswing from start to finish.
- Don't let your left arm collapse when it starts the downswing. Always keep your left arm extended straight and keep pushing it out as far away from your head as possible for the entire downswing. This will help to keep your left arm straight and to make a smooth & well rounded downswing.
- As soon as the downswing starts it is very important to immediately keep your hands in front of your chest and to stay there for the entire of the downswing. You don't want your hands falling too far behind or getting too far ahead. You want your hands to stay in front of your chest at all times and turn in synchronization with your upper-body and shoulders.
- Don't let your shoulders unwind faster than your arms. Make sure your arms unwind at the same speed as all other parts & move down together to form a synchronized downswing.
- Make sure your arms feel asleep and feel like dead weight. The only thing you feel is the clubhead swinging around you. Your arms, hands & clubshaft feel like a piece of rope being swung around your body with a pail of water tied to the end of it, the clubhead. That's how round and perfect you want your golf swing to feel.

Shoulders

- Your right shoulder is turning, uncoiling smoothly and deliberately trying to get to the slot under your chin.

Head

- Your head is not sliding forward. It is dead still & very steady getting ready for impact.
- Make sure you keep your head well behind the ball throughout the entire downswing.
- Your head does not move up or down even the tiniest little bit.
- Keep your chin held up high for the entire downswing.

Back

- Unwind your hips on a swivel. Don't slide them towards the target.
- Make sure you unwind your upper-body on a swivel too. It is not a sliding motion, it is a definite unwinding. Don't slide towards the target even one millimeter throughout the entire downswing.
- Start unwinding your hips early on before you start unwinding your shoulders. Your hips need an early start to make sure they will be whipping through the hitting zone by the time all the other parts gets there.
- You are trying to clear the left side of your body out of the way to let the right side of your body through.

Legs

- Push off your back right knee just a little bit to start the downswing. Remember, you are unwinding from the ground up, so your back right leg starts the downswing.
- Your back right knee is flexed releasing all of its power and your front left leg is braced getting ready to receive all the weight transfer.
- Keep both of your legs flexed to maintain a stable base.

Feet

- Immediately start shifting all of your weight gently but surely towards your front left foot as soon as the downswing starts.
- Keep your left heel grounded, the whole sole of your front left foot is flat on the ground for the entire downswing.

- Your back right foot twists up and your back right heel starts to come off the ground.

Overall

- The motion in your downswing needs to flow in the correct sequence.
- You want the clubhead to come swinging in from the inside, down the aimline, then back inside again. An inside-to-square-to-inside swinging clubhead path is the flow you want your clubhead to travel down and through the hitting zone.

Transferring To The Next Stage

- Your hands and clubhead & shoulders are now all lined up with each other just in time directly in front of you at the bottom of the downswing. They are in the same position that they were in at address swishing through the hitting zone freely.
- Your arms and hands are still asleep, just dead weight being whipped around your body by the turning force and weight of the swinging clubhead like a pail of water tied to the end of a rope.

The Downswing Process

- Unwinding is like a spring, don't over swing the club. All you do is unwind like a spring does. Be as mechanically perfect & as particular as you can be. Swing in your most natural and smoothest rhythm possible.
- The only time you can start the aggressive acceleration for full power is at the bottom arc of the downswing once your hands get below hip height. At this point, make sure you do accelerate purposely and always thwack through the hitting zone forcefully.
- You are fully coiled up at the top of the fullswing and simply unwinding your body in the smoothest & roundness way possible in the downswing. Remember, you are uncoiling, not sliding your body towards the target.
- The downswing always starts from the ground up. Start the downswing by unwinding your lower-body first. Your lower-body

leads your upper-body. Your upper-body leads your arms. Your arms lead your hands. Your hands lead the clubhead until everything catches up with each other just in time for the thwack through the hitting zone.

Downswing Order
- Firstly, start shifting your weight off your back right leg.
- Secondly, start unwinding & turning your hips.
- Thirdly, start unwinding & turning your shoulders.
- Fourthly, your arms come back around.
- Lastly, the clubhead comes back around.

Top Of Downswing (First Part)
- The start of the downswing needs to begin slowly, smoothly and gently just like you started the swing in the takeway. Don't force the clubhead downwards, let it fall into place before you purposely start swinging the clubhead around.
- It's a brief lazy feeling. Have patience, wait for it, don't rush the swing downwards. Don't jerk the downswing trying to start it forwards. Flow with the natural momentum of the swing.
- Your lower-body starts the downswing turning & unwinding rather quickly to get a head start on your upper-body. Your lower-body leads everything else in the top half of the swing down and through.

Bottom Of Downswing (Second Part)
- At the bottom part of the downswing your arms & hands are still asleep & very quiet. You are releasing the clubhead with no hand or arm muscles pulling & no tension whatsoever.
- Gradually build up more and more speed, flow with it, accelerate constantly & purposely until you are unwinding very fast and deliberately swishing through the bottom part of the downswing forcefully.
- Your upper-body is lagging and has fallen behind, it doesn't unwind too much in the first part of the downswing. Don't start unwinding your upper-body parts until your hands get to around

hip height. At this point, in the bottom part of the downswing the top-half of your body needs to unwind faster than the lower-half of your body in order to catch up. Then, everything will be lined up square in front of you just as they were setup at address as you make it to impact with the ball.

(A-7) Hitting Zone

Club & Ball

- The correct swinging flow of your clubhead through the hitting zone for a perfectly straight shot is inside-to-square-to-inside. On the way through the hitting zone, the exact middle of your clubhead starts inside the aimline and swings out just to the aimline, spending virtually no time there at all for the moment of impact with the ball, and then the exact middle of your clubhead swings back inside the aimline again. Although the swing will feel like you are swinging straight down the aimline the whole way through the hitting zone.

- Make sure you keep the clubface square to your left forearm throughout the entire swing. Although, the clubface will come down the aimline looking open, just makes it to square at impact, and goes down the aimline closing as you release your hands and forearms over. The clubface is only ever square to the ball at the exact moment of impact, but it is square to your left forearm for the entire swing. The clubface only sneaks in there square to the ball for just a split second, just in time at the moment of impact.

- Make sure you always line up the exact center point of the clubface with the exact center point of the golf ball to maximize the speed, quality & accuracy of your shot. Aim for perfection. Concentrate & focus on this exact center needlepoint in the middle of the clubface nailing into the exact center needlepoint on the back of the ball for all your swings.

- For all swings hit the ball first, then turf second. The only exception is the driver which is a level & pure sweeping motion that hits the ball off a raised tee.

- The higher the iron, the steeper you need to descend down into the ball for a crisp & straighter shot. Swinging down into the ball is actually what causes the ball to pop up.
- The ball is just an object that gets in the way of your perfect swinging clubhead. Forget that the ball is even there as you swing through the hitting zone. Concentrate on your mechanics & smooth rhythm. Don't think of the ball as an object to hit, think of the ball as a target point to focus on.
- Don't hit at the ball or try to guide your clubhead through the hitting zone. Just unwind naturally and freely through impact, don't tense up.
- There always needs to be a free flowing swish sound as you release the clubhead through the hitting zone.
- The clubhead has been lagging way behind, catching up this whole time and just catches up in time at the moment of impact. It feels like the clubhead is coming in so slow that it won't make it through on time, but it does, it whips through just in time like a pail of water does being whipped around your body tied to the end of a rope.
- It is more of a cupping the ball feeling through impact than slicing the ball feeling for all shots, even the driver. Make sure the clubface is square to the ball through impact and keep your hands well ahead of the clubhead through impact for crisper & straighter shots.
- Make sure the clubshaft is tilted forwards, angled towards the target all the way through the hitting zone. This will also slightly decrease the natural loft of the clubface at impact. The ball won't pop up as high and will fly & roll a little farther than normal. But, this is the crisp & straight shot that you want.

Hands

- Make sure your hands are ahead of the clubhead and keep your right palm facing 90 degrees downwards through the entire hitting zone.
- Your wrists finish fully unhinging just in time at the point of impact making a thwack through the hitting zone.

- Rotate your hands through the hitting zone in order to release the clubhead freely & squarely through impact. In other words, your right hand rolls over your left hand.
- Keep your hands asleep, dead quiet, tension free & don't tighten them up through the hitting zone. Keep them at the same light grip pressure that you started with at address. Just continue with the flow and consciously & gently push your right hand evenly and smoothly towards the target.
- Don't fling at the ball with your hands or become too wristy through impact. Let your wrists flow through the hitting zone & unhinge naturally.
- Make sure your hands are still ahead of the ball at impact to make sure you squeeze the shot for a cleaner and more crisp & solid shot.
- The higher the club and more descending the swing, the farther ahead of the clubhead your hands need to be at impact, such as for short-irons & wedge shots. The lower the club and more sweeping the swing, the less ahead of the clubhead your hands need to be at impact, such as for long-irons & the driver. But, your hands always need to be ahead of the clubhead for every single swing you make.

Arms

- Squeeze your forearms towards each other & keep them strongly flexed & caved in towards each other through the entire hitting zone.
- Think of trying to touch your forearms together to help squeeze the swing nice & tight through impact and for a more crisp & solid shot.
- Also squeeze your elbows as close together as you can throughout the entire hitting zone.
- Rotate your forearms through the hitting zone. In other words, your right forearm rolls over your left forearm.
- Both of your arms are stretched to their maximum and are extended as long & straight as they can be away from you. They are sturdy & whipping through the hitting zone very quickly by the turning & swinging force of your uncoiling body.

- Keep your right elbow tucked in as close as you can to the right side of your body. You don't want your arms flying out & away from you, keep your arms turning in nice & tight.
- Make sure your right elbow is in front of your right hip throughout the entire hitting zone.

Shoulders

- Right shoulder is smoothly turning quickly on its way into the slot under your chin.
- Both of your shoulders just make it to perfectly square at impact and are facing directly in front of you the same way they were at address. Your shoulders are not slightly angled backwards or slightly angled forwards, but your shoulders are looking directly straight in front of you perfectly parallel to your aimline at impact.

Head

- Your head is at the exact same height it was at address. It hasn't bounced up or down even a millimeter.
- Chin is still held up high.
- Your head is totally still and stays well behind the ball through impact. Don't let your head slide forward and through the hitting zone until well into the followthrough.
- Keep your eyes focused on the needlepoint in the middle of the back of the golf ball trying to match it up with the needlepoint on the middle of your clubface. Also, think about where you are going to start the perfect divot mark. The perfect divot mark starts just in front of the ball, not behind it, because you always hit the ball first, then turf second.

Back

- You are trying to clear your left side quickly out of the way, therefore your left side and hips are the first parts to enter the followthrough. Whip your lower-body and hips around so quickly that they are cleared well out of the way by impact.

- Your upper-body is not sliding forward but stays in one place behind the golf ball, unwinding smoothly & fiercely on a swivel through the hitting zone.
- Spine angle is tilted back away from the target and also leaning slightly forwards towards the ground, the same angle as it was at address. It still hasn't changed.
- Upper-body is perfectly square and facing directly in front of you parallel to the aimline at impact.

Legs
- Both legs are very flexed to maintain a stable base, especially a very stable front left leg & knee through impact.

Feet
- All weight & momentum of the swing is now balanced and in the middle of your body, but all weight is quickly & strongly being transferred towards your front left foot.

Overall
- Your arms are reaching, stretching out in front of you in full extension by impact.
- Keep pulling your body and hands away from the ball though to keep as far away from the ball as you can though the hitting zone. You want to make sure you are fully extended through impact.
- You will be swinging at your fastest an 85% of full power swing by the time you get to impact. Never swing harder than 85% for any swing, not even for the driver.
- Make sure the bottom half of every swing is deliberate & solid, in control & smooth, but always accelerating aggressively. Never slow down through the hitting zone, no matter how short the swing is. All swings at impact need to be an unleashing of forward momentum.
- Let everything go with the flow through the hitting zone. Let your instincts take over.

- It takes a while to build up momentum & speed in a swing, so don't force it, let it build up gradually & naturally. The top speed of your swing will always be at the bottom arc of your swing, so don't rush it, it'll get there.

Transferring To The Next Stage
- Thwack yourself through the bottom arc of the swing quite aggressively like you are swooshing a whip or like you are thwacking your clubhead into the back of a spare tire lying on the ground in front of you.

(A-8) Followthrough

Club & Ball
- Immediately after impact with the ball, the toe of your clubface starts turning over the heel. In other words, you are releasing the clubhead freely.
- At the end of the followthrough your clubshaft is above & behind your head pointing in the complete opposite direction of your target on a parallel line to your aimline hanging & swaying in the wind with the toe of the clubface pointing straight down towards the ground. In other words, the clubface is still square to your left forearm.
- The clubshaft & your hands are not touching your body, they are high up in the air & away from you, just hanging in the wind.

Hands
- When your right arm swings back up to horizontal and is level to the ground again pointing directly at the target, both of your thumbs will be pointing straight up to the sky 90 degrees for descending swings & only be pointing 45 degrees of way up for sweeping swings. In other words, your wrists have fully hinged by then for descending swings, and only half hinged back up for sweeping swings.

- Your right hand rotates over your left hand immediately after impact to make sure there is a free release of the clubhead.
- Your hands will be freewheeling through the hitting zone in order to release the clubhead & to make sure the clubhead always whips down the aimline after impact.

Arms

- Keep your forearms flexed and caved in towards each other well into the followthrough.
- It still feels like your elbows are touching all the way through the followthrough.
- Your arms will be freewheeling through the hitting zone. Keep them loose and extended as straight as you can for as long as you can in the first part of the followthrough. They will eventually & naturally bend upwards and break apart in the final part of the followthrough.

Shoulders

- Right shoulder ends up fully turned & under the slot of your chin by the end of the followthrough.
- Your right shoulder whips through the hitting zone & your whole body and right shoulder finally slide through the hitting zone & end up so far forward that your back right shoulder is lined up directly over your front left knee by the final part of the followthrough.

Head

- Your head stays at the exact same height it was at for the entire swing all the way into the final part of the followthrough. It never moves up or down, not even a millimeter.
- Your head will eventually move, but not up or down, it will get pulled through the hitting zone by the swinging force & momentum of the swing and your head will end up so far forward that it'll be lined up over your front left knee by the final part of the followthrough.

- Keep your head back for as long as you possibly can though. Consciously hold your head back in place until it has no choice but to get pulled through the hitting zone.
- Your head is the last thing that gets pulled through the hitting zone.

Back

- Make sure your upper-body & lower-body have fully turned through the swing.
- If you are wearing a belt, your belt buckle will be facing directly at the target by the final part of the followthrough.
- Your spine angle still needs to be relatively upright and straight by the end of the followthrough. Your height never changes. You haven't bounced up or down at all. All you did was wind up and unwind fiercely on a swivel like the unwinding of a spring.

Legs

- All of the weight of your body ends up on your front left leg.
- Both legs remain flexed all the way through the swing so that you still have a stable base all the way to the end of the followthrough.
- Your front left knee becomes super braced as it collects all the weight coming in from your right side.

Feet

- Almost all of your weight ends up on the outside of your front left foot.
- Your back right heel has to let go of all weight and will twist turn up loosely until your right foot is pointing straight down on a 90 degree angle to the ground. In other words, your right toes are pointing to the ground & your left foot still hasn't moved at all. (Note: Your front left foot may have no choice but to turn open a bit towards the target by the aggressive turning force of the swing, but the whole sole of your front left foot, both heels & toes always remain flat on the ground for the entire swing from address to followthrough)

Overall

- In the first part of the followthrough everything is freewheeling through.
- In the final part of the followthrough it is all about collecting and maintaining your balance for a picture perfect three second pause.
- All of your weight has now moved to your left side.

Transferring To The Next Stage

- Keep your balance. Don't fall towards the target & don't rush out of the final picture perfect finish for approximately three seconds.
- Bring the golf club down slowly.
- Walk out of your stance and away from the shot slowly.
- Do everything slowly and unrushed, calm, cool & collectively.

(A-9) Overall

Club & Ball

- The clubface needs to stay square to your left forearm throughout the entire swing. Make sure you can feel the correct position of the square clubface in all points during the swing.
- On the backswing, the butt-end of your club handle points & trails just in front of your toes for descending type swings & points & trails more in the middle area between your toes and the ball for sweeping type swings.
- On the downswing, the butt-end of your club handle points slightly farther out than it did on the backswing. On the downswing, the butt-end of your club handle points & trails more towards the ball for descending type swings & points & trails just outside the ball for sweeping type swings.

Hands

- Always concentrate on your hands and on feeling the clubhead with your hands throughout the entire swing from address to

followthrough. Concentrating on feeling your hands will improve your rhythm, timing & smoothness.
- Your hands need to be fully relaxed, quiet, almost asleep, free flowing with absolutely no tension at all, especially through the hitting zone.
- Keep your grip pressure light & constant, equal pressure throughout the entire swing from address to followthrough. Especially make sure & concentrate on not tightening your left control hand throughout the entire swing.
- Concentrate on keeping your pinkie finger on your left hand from not loosening and the next two fingers up will stay firm as well. This way you'll be able to keep a good hold of the club handle easily with such a light grip pressure.

Both Hands Work As One
- Both hands try their best to work together as one unit, but each hand does have its own individual purpose & function.

Left Hand
- Your left hand is the hand that takes most of the control throughout the swing.
- Your left hand is the hand that helps to swing the swinging clubhead towards the target squarely.
- Your left hand is the hand that holds the club firmly in the last three fingers of this right hand.
- Your left hand controls the hinging of the clubshaft and wrists throughout the entire swing.
- Your left hand helps determine how much to descend or sweep into the back of the ball.

Right Hand
- Your right hand doesn't do much of anything at all. It is just the hand that follows or gets pulled along for the ride.
- Your right hand's sole purpose is to flow & only to help accelerate a touch of power in the bottom of the downswing.

Arms

- Your arms control your shoulders throughout the entire swing. It is the complete opposite of the putting swing where your upper-back & abdominal muscles control the putting swing. In the fullswing, it is a very aggressive arm controlled swing with a fast turning body that enables you to strike the ball so far.
- Keep your elbows consistently close together for the entire swing from address to followthrough. This will keep the swing tight & compact. Don't let your elbows get away from each other or the swing will become loose & sloppy.
- Always keep your right elbow tucked in as close as you can to the right side of your body, don't let it open up or get away from you. Your right elbow has the feeling like it is almost connected to your right hip.

Back

- Keep your spine angle at the exact same constant angle throughout the entire swing from address to followthrough.
- The hub of your swing is somewhere in the middle of your shoulders, just below your shoulder blades. This is the center point, the balancing hub that everything turns & revolves around on a swivel.
- Don't get lazy or forget and make half attempts at shoulder rotations back & forth through the swing. Make sure you always make a full upper-body rotation in the backswing and a full upper-body rotation in the followthrough.

Shoulders

- Make sure it is a full 90 degree shoulder turn on the backswing and a full 90 degree shoulder turn on the followthrough for all fullswings.

Head

- Your head can also be considered the hub of the swing. Keep your head in the middle of your body for the entire swing until the final part of the followthrough when it is the last body part that has no choice, but to get pulled through the hitting zone as well.

- Don't let your head move up or down for the entire swing though. No swaying or bouncing your head all around, it needs to stay in place very level & at the same height from address to followthrough.
- Keep your chin up high well up off your chest for the entire swing from address to followthrough so that your left shoulder has lots of room to get under your chin in the backswing & your right shoulder has lots of room to get under your chin in the downswing.
- Wind everything around your head. Think of your head as a piece of machinery that is fixed in place and doesn't move. Concentrate on a smooth swing winding up and around your head like your head is the center of it all.
- Keeping your head steady & at the exact same height throughout the entire swing is probably one of the most important fundamentals there is.
- Keep your head perfectly still and revolve everything else around it which keeps everything throughout your swing centered and online.
- Your eyes are always concentrating and focused on the very middle needle-point point on the back of the golf ball and on the exact middle needle-point of your clubface making contact with each other for the most perfect crisp & accurate swing you can make.

Legs

- Both of your legs are always slightly flexed & balanced and in the ready position for the entire swing from address to followthrough.
- Keep both of your knees firm & braced for the entire swing to keep a solid foundation and to hold everything up for the entire swing.
- Your legs are relaxed and not dramatic. Keep your leg action quiet. Don't have your legs bending and swinging all over the place.

Feet

- Keep your front left heel grounded throughout the entire swing from address to followthrough. It's the back right heel that eventually comes off the ground in the downswing & ends up pointing into the ground at a 90 degree angle by the end of the followthrough.
- In the backswing, almost all of your body weight shifts towards your back right foot. In the downswing, almost all your body weight shifts towards your front left foot. Keep your weight shift in rhythm & harmony with the direction of your swinging hands & clubhead.

Overall

- All of your fullswing shots should be swung at a maximum of 85% of full power and no more. Rarely swing a club at 90% of full power and definitely never ever put everything you got into a swing and swing at 100% of full power. Not even for the driver! 85% of full power is always the maximum amount of power you should ever be swinging at.
- Swing at the exact same rhythm & tempo that is comfortable for you. Keep it constant & consistent and swing at the same speed each and every time.
- Keeping your swing in control is extremely important, so always keep it in control. But, never let up on a swing trying to get too fancy or touchy. It needs to be a forward momentum, aggressive, positive & solid release of the clubhead for every single swing you make no matter how long or short the swing is.
- Really concentrate on keeping every part of your body relaxed & comfortable. There can't be any strain anywhere, don't let any tension get into any part of your body.
- Really concentrate on keeping everything up during the entire swing. You are a tall & erect structure. Don't slouch, don't take short cuts & don't make lazy swings. Stay alert & always keep the swing up. Keep everything up, up, up.
- Your weight needs to flow in the same smooth direction that the clubhead is travelling in throughout the entire swing. In other words, all of your weight shifts to the right side of your body in

the backswing and all of your weight shifts to the left side of your body in the downswing.

- You want to try and create every single swing you make to be the most eloquent, maximum energy, fluidness, smooth & accurate swing you can make it.

Synchronize Arm-Swing & Body-Turn

- Your arms swinging around your body stay connected with your body-turn. They stay in harmony & are synchronized with each other.
- Don't let them break out of line with each other. Keep your hands and arms in front of your body for all points during the swing. Don't let your arms fall too far behind or swing too far ahead.
- Your shoulder turn is perfectly blended with your arms swinging throughout the entire swing from address to followthrough.
- Swing in your exact same unique & distinct style every single time. Don't change it. Your swing can't be going at this tempo one day and that tempo another day. Swing your club in the exact same way every single day.
- Feel your body rotating in harmony with the swinging motion of your arms, hands & clubhead.

(B)
Three Other Swings

(B-1) Finesse Short Game Swing

The Grip

- The finesse grip is very similar to the main fundamental fullswing grip, but this grip is an even weaker & lighter grip.
- Your hands are square and are not twisting in on each other like they are in the fullswing grip.
- Hold and control the club even more in your fingers than you do in the fullswing.
- The crease on both your right hand & left hand made between your thumb and forefinger will both be pointing directly at your nose for a weak grip. You will only be able to see approximately 1.5 knuckles on each hand.
- This is the softest grip you can possibly hold a club with while still maintaining control and still holding the club sturdy.
- Both of your hands will be lined up square to each other & exactly parallel to each other. Both hands will also be square with the clubface.

Address

- Ball position is in the exact middle of your stance for all finesse swings.
- Stance is very narrow with only approximately 18 inches of space between the inside of your feet. This is so that you can control the swing better & control it more with your body, not with your hands & arms.
- Keep everything in your stance square to the aimline, but open your front left foot approximately 45 degrees towards the target.

This will help to encourage your hips to clear & turn quickly through the hitting zone.

- Stand a little taller and a little closer to the ball than you would for a fullswing. You only need to bend over just a touch to allow your shoulders to turn back & forth smoothly.
- Don't cave your forearms in towards each other like you do in the fullswing.
- Your hands are square and forearms are relaxed.
- Your hands and arms are even more loose and quiet than for a fullswing.

Takeaway

- Take away everything together as usual in one synchronized motion to start the swing.
- Don't let your arms start the swinging motion. Let your lower-body & upper-body turn back together at the exact same time.
- Your arms, hands and fingers are totally asleep and feel dead quiet.

Backswing

- The finesse swing doesn't go up and into the perfect box structure like the fullswing does. The farthest you ever swing back is ¾ of the way at most because your upper-body doesn't coil around your lower-body in this swing. Everything stops at ¾ of the way there in the backswing and everything comes back down and through at the exact same time.
- The finesse swing is much more vertical going up in the backswing than horizontal going around your body like in the fullswing.
- Keep the backswing as short as you can. Don't let it go back farther than necessary. You don't need an overly long backswing. This is a finesse swing, not a power swing. You lose some distance, but gain accuracy.
- Keep your hands and clubhead in even tighter on the backswing than in the fullswing. Do not let your arms swing out and around you. Keep the turn tight & compact.

- Your shoulders turn back steeply upwards. Remember, don't turn your shoulders around your body like in the fullswing, the backswing needs to be quite steep & vertical.
- Turn your lower-body & upper-body at the exact same time. They are perfectly synchronized for the entire finesse swing from address to followthrough. You do not coil your upper-body around your lower-body like you do in the fullswing. In other words, don't swing your arms behind you and coil your arms around your chest.
- Your hips turn together in synchronization with everything else as well. Keep turning everything back together until your hips stop turning at a full 45 degrees and that is when everything else stops turning as well.
- For the descending type swings in the fullswing you hinge your wrists rather quickly in the backswing. In the finesse swing, don't start hinging your wrists too quickly, but gradually and continuously. Your wrists don't finish fully hinging up until the very top of the finesse backswing.

Top Of Backswing

- It needs to be a slow & patient transition from the backswing to the downswing the same as in the fullswing. There needs to be a lag.

Downswing

- Slowly, but constantly keep increasing the speed throughout the entire downswing from start to finish. Never slow down or let up on the swing trying to get too fancy or touchy. You always need a solid & positive increasing speed of the clubhead through impact for all swings.
- Your lower-body does not lead your upper-body through the downswing like it does in the fullswing. Both upper-body & lower-body come down and through at the exact same time.
- The power for the finesse swing comes from your shoulders & upper-body, not from your arms muscling around like in the fullswing.

Hitting Zone

- Your hands & forearms still rotate through the hitting zone to release the clubhead. In otherwords, your right hand & forearm rotate over your left hand & forearm.
- The clubhead needs to come through the hitting zone aggressively, solidly & positively.
- Keep your hands and arms as soft & asleep as possible to help you feel the distance of the shot you are trying to make.
- The lowest point of the finesse swing arc will always be in the exact same place in the very middle of your feet for every single swing no matter how long or short the swing is. Therefore, position the ball approximately two inches behind this middle point so that you always make a crisp ball first, then turf second contact.
- Your perfectly synchronized swing will allow you to hit the exact same location in the very middle of your feet over and over again consistently without having to control your arms & hands. You want to swing into the same place in the very middle of your feet for every single finesse swing you make.
- Keep your front left leg as straight & tall as it can be through impact. But, not too firm, it still needs to be relaxed & comfortable.

Followthrough

- Make sure the finesse swing followthrough is approximately 50% longer than the backswing was. It's a very high & full finish.
- It is not a low followthrough with the hands like in a fullswing. The hands rise much steeper and much higher in the followthrough.
- No matter how long or short the finesse swing is make sure all your weight transfers fully to your front left foot in the followthrough.
- Your left hand should almost touch your left ear at the very end of a full finesse swing followthrough.

Overall

- This is a much simpler swing, therefore there is a lot less chance of something breaking down while you swing. Since the top of the backswing is only ¾ of the way back, and everything goes back and through together, it makes for a much easier & smoother transition from backswing to downswing.

- Turn your upper-body & lower-body in synchronization at the exact same time from start to finish. There is no coiling up in the finesse swing. Your upper-body & lower-body turn back & forth as if they were literally connected.

- You need the exact same super smooth tempo, relaxed & natural rhythm for every single finesse swing you make.

- The finesse swing is a feel & touch swing for ultimate distance & control. It is a very accurate & straight pitching swing that is very consistent at controlling distances.

- The finesse swing is still a solid & forward momentum swing, but a much more lazy feeling swing at the same time. It is a low power swing. It is not a power swing like the fullswing.

- Concentrate even more with this swing to feel the swinging clubhead with your hands in order to help control the distance of the shot better.

- Don't hinge your wrists up early in the backswing and wait to unleash them in the downswing like you do in the fullswing. Let your wrists flow naturally up & down gradually like a carpenter hammering a nail.

- Your wrists hinge & unhinge with the natural momentum of the swing. Your hands & wrists don't add any power to the swing like they do in the fullswing, they just flow.

- Your hands, arms & forearms are asleep & super loose, zero tension and pure dead weight similar to the putting swing. They are just dead weight being swung around in natural rhythm with the turning motion of your shoulders & upper-body.

- Keep your right arm extended straight as can be throughout the entire swing. Don't let it bend much at the elbow like it does in the fullswing. As always, do the same thing with your left arm as well.

- The distance you want the ball to go is controlled by the backswing length. The exact same as the putting swing.

- You are a swinging clock that is controlled much more with your shoulders than your arms. Your left shoulder is the center of the clock & your left arm is the hour hand. Don't use your clubshaft as the hour hand to determine swing lengths.
- 7 O'clock = ¼ finesse backswing: Hands just past right knee.
- 8 O'clock = ½ finesse backswing: Hands just below hips.
- 9 O'clock = ¾ finesse backswing: Hands just above hip height & left arm level & horizontal to the ground.
- 10 O'clock = A full backswing for the finesse swing (3/4 of a fullswing): Hands up around neck height.

(B-2) Chipping Swing

The Chipping Grip
- The chipping grip is also very similar to the main fundamental fullswing grip, but it is firmer & with your left hand turned way open.
- The right hand grip on the club handle is the same as for the finesse grip. The crease on your right hand made between your thumb and forefinger will be pointing directly at your nose. You will see approximately 1.5 knuckles on this right hand. It will also be square to the clubface.
- Your left hand is turned way open. It is back on itself almost under the club handle so that you can't even see a knuckle on it or barely see one knuckle at the most.
- The grip pressure is a bit firmer than normal so that the clubhead won't turn closed at impact. But, you still need a light & soft hand grip in order to feel & judge the distance of your shots better.
- Take off your golf glove and use just your bare hands for added touch and feel. The same as you would do when putting.

Address
- Turn & open your whole stance about 20 degrees to the left of the target. Everything, both feet, knees, hips, shoulders & eyes are all 20 degrees opened to the left of the target.

- Pull your front left foot back just a touch from the aimline so that your hips can easily turn through the swing.
- Ball position is all the way back in your stance to align just inside your back right foot. Never position the ball any farther back than this though or you'll create too much backspin & make too many mishits.
- Everything is open 20 degrees to the left of the target, but make sure your clubface is square and aimed directly at the target. The clubface is not 20 degrees open to the left like everything else is. The clubface may even seem closed, but it's not, it's square to the target.
- You can even open the clubface slightly for higher & softer chip shots.
- Your hands are far forward to line up just inside your front left knee and therefore the clubshaft will be tilted very forward towards the target.
- The clubface is delofted quite a few degrees which helps to punch the ball forward and get the ball rolling.
- Don't choke down on the grip. That will encourage a flatter angle of attack with less backspin. You want to make sure it's a crisp & descending angle of attack into the back of the ball each and every time.
- Sit down a bit more than you would for a regular fullswing. Your knees are bent more than normal and both knees are tilted slightly to the left towards the target.
- Super narrow stance. Only have 4 to 6 inches of space between the inside of your feet.
- Stand as close as you possibly can to the ball.
- Stand as tall as you possibly can. A feeling very tall and erect stance is still needed.
- Bend your wrists to the left towards the target, tilt them forwards for chipping swings.
- 35% of your weight is on your back right back foot / 65% of your weight is on your front left foot. Your weight distribution is more on your front left foot to make sure it is a slightly more descending blow into the back of the ball than for a regular fullswing.
- Raise your hands up a touch higher than normal to keep them firm.

- Keep the bottom of your clubface up a bit off the ground to make sure you'll hit the ball first, then turf second through the hitting zone. In other words, don't rest your clubhead on an eggshell like you do in the fullswing, have it even higher off the ground than this.

Backswing

- Sweep the clubhead back and keep it low to the ground for the first 12 inches and then it starts to go upwards quite steeply after that.
- Bring the clubhead directly straight back, not to the inside on the takeaway.
- Make a shorter & more compact backswing than normal.
- Keep your left arm fully extended the whole way back, don't bend your left elbow at all.
- Don't takeaway with just your hands. Sweep the clubhead away in a gentle rocking movement of your shoulders & only use a touch of hand power. Then, use mostly your hands and arm muscles in the rest of the backswing, but maintain the connection to your turning shoulders.
- Don't forget to turn your shoulders & rotate your body even for the shortest chips. Think of having a second golf club lodged up under your armpits and rock it back and forth without letting the golf club fall out is the correct chipping technique to have.
- Your wrists don't ever fully hinge, but do hinge slightly to help bring the club up on the backswing.
- As always, your head does not move back or up or down even a millimeter. Keep it dead still for the entire backswing.
- Keep your weight distributed with 35% on your back right foot / 65% on your front left foot for the entire backswing. Don't transfer your weight to your back right foot like you do in a fullswing or a finesse swing.
- Never make more than a 3/4 backswing, no further. Club up & swing easy for farther chipping distance.

Top Of Backswing

- Keep your hands and wrists soft & light during the transition to the downswing.
- You want everything to lag for a split second before the downswing starts. The exact same as in every other swing.

Downswing

- The clubhead flows down the aimline and into the ball only slightly from the inside.
- Your left wrist is flowing straight down the aimline and online with the target. Keep your left arm firm.
- Concentrate on keeping your hands & wrists quiet, not the unleashing of your wrists like in a regular fullswing.
- Keep your hands even more ahead of the clubhead for the entire downswing than you would for a regular fullswing.
- Aim to hit steeply downwards on the ball.
- Don't forget to turn your body. Turn your chest towards the target.
- Keep a very stable base with your legs, perhaps even more than for a regular fullswing. Keep your legs very quiet, don't have your legs moving much at all.

Hitting Zone

- Everything will be back in the exact same position as it was at address for the moment of impact. Think about re-creating the exact same address position in your mind as you strike the ball.
- The clubface needs to be perfectly square at impact to make sure there is no sidespin created that will affect the roll of the ball.
- The clubhead comes in on a shallow angle of attack low to the ground through impact. It's a sweeping motion, but it's definitely a descending strike in order to hit the ball first, then turf second. Don't try to scoop the ball up in the air, the downward strike will pop the ball up.
- A very thin divot needs to be taken, but not a deep divot like in the fullswing.

- Don't stop or slow down through the hitting zone. It's a delicate shot, but a positive & solid free releasing of the clubhead is still needed.
- Keep your left hand comfortable & relaxed but firm through the hitting zone.
- Your hands are still way ahead of the clubhead.
- Keep your head dead steady and keep looking down at the ball the same as you would for a putt.
- Delay releasing the clubhead for as long as possible because the clubhead is so far behind your hands. You want the clubhead to hit the ball first, then release the clubhead second. At this point, as always, release your hands, forearms and clubface through impact. In other words, your right hand & forearm rotate over your left hand & forearm.

Followthrough

- The followthrough is just a touch longer than your backswing, but definitely longer.
- Your clubhead and hands stay low to the ground in the finish.

Overall

- Your wrists stay at the same angle for the entire swing, similar to the putting swing. Your wrists stay soft, yet are firm and only hinge slightly. Your wrists don't break down. There is no wrist action like in a regular fullswing or finesse swing.
- Make sure you still use a fairly light hand grip with dead quiet hands, but also keep the grip firm at the same time. Don't use your hands or wrists for power.
- Your lower-body stays very quiet and doesn't move much at all. There is very little leg movement. It's a complete upper-body swing.
- There is no body power, no arm power and no wrist power. It's just a smooth swinging motion back & forth similar to the putting swing.
- Keep your head & upper-body well behind the ball until well after impact.

- Keep your head dead steady and don't let it bounce up or down or back even a millimeter. It stays in the exact same place and at the exact same height throughout the entire swing.
- Keep 35% of your weight on your back right foot / 65% of your weight on your front left foot for the entire swing.
- Turn your shoulders in synchronization & harmony with the movement of your hands, arms and clubhead in front of you. There is no coiling up.
- You need a smooth & free swinging of the arms, shoulders, and hips all synchronized together for a perfect & delicate chip shot. Keep it slow and easy, there is no need to rush through the swing. If you need to hit the ball farther, simply take a longer & smoother swing or club up & swing easy.
- The clubhead stays pretty much online with the aimline for the entire swing. Slightly inside-to-square-to-inside, similar to a long lag putt for a putting swing.
- The swing is controlled more by your upper-back & abdominal muscles than by your arms and hands, similar to the putting swing.
- Keep a constant triangle intact for the entire swing. Your shoulders and both arms form a triangle. Your arms are the two sides of the triangle and the line across your shoulders are the third side. Keep the triangle intact and constant while swinging in synchronization with your body turn. Don't let this triangle break down for the entire chipping swing from address to followthrough. In other words, don't bend your elbows. It's very similar to the putting swing.

(B-3) Greenside Splash Sand Bunker Swing

The Greenside Splash Sand Bunker Grip

- The splash sand bunker grip has a lot of similarities to the main fundamental fullswing grip, but it is a very firm grip & a very open grip that gets you ready to slice into the sand under the ball.
- Open the clubface 45 degrees to the right of the target.

- Your right hand grips the club the same way as you would for a finesse swing grip or a chipping swing grip. The crease on your right hand made between your thumb and forefinger will be pointing directly at your nose. You will see approximately 1.5 knuckles on this right hand. It will also be square to the clubface.
- Your left hand is turned open so much to the left that you can't see any knuckles on it at all. The back of your left hand is pretty much under the club handle.
- Keep a fairly firm grip on the club handle. This is one of the most aggressive swings you'll have to make on the golf course.

Address

- Open your clubface so much that it is aimed approximately 45 degrees to the right of the target and everything else is lined up approximately 45 degrees to the left of the target.
- Open everything up in your stance, your feet, knees, hips, shoulders, and eyes so that you are aligned approximately 45 degrees to the left of target.
- Where you are aligned is also the same aimline that you swing down.
- Hover the clubhead just above the sand. You are not allowed to touch the sand before the swing starts or during the backswing or you'll receive a one stroke penalty for doing so.
- 50% of your weight is on your back right foot / 50% of you weight is on your front left foot.
- Position the ball very forward in your stance so it is aligned just inside your front left foot. You want the ball forward in your stance so that the clubhead can slide under the ball on a shallow angle of attack and make the necessary splash.
- Shuffle your feet down into the sand to give yourself a solid base and to feel what the texture of the sand is like.
- Keep the stance fairly narrow with only approximately 18 inches of space between your feet.
- Choke down on the grip handle because your feet will be sunk into the sand & you will be a little lower to the ground than normal.
- Lower your hands quite a bit more towards the ground than you would for a fullswing. In other words, push the heel of the club

down and the toe of the club lifts up in the air. This helps the bounce work better on the bottom front edge of your sandwedge. It makes sure you'll have a smooth slide through the sand & create the necessary splash.

- Your hands are not too far ahead of the ball, just a touch ahead of the ball is necessary.

Backswing

- Take the clubhead back along the aimline along your feet. In other words, you take the clubhead back diagonally away from the target line on a 45 degree angle well to the outside.
- You need it to be a very wide one-piece takeaway to the outside to make sure the clubhead will come back down in the downswing swinging severely to the inside.
- Rotate your forearms back quickly & almost immediately to the right to open the clubface even more as you swing back.
- Start hinging your wrists quickly as well to encourage a steep backswing. Your wrists should be fully hinged as early as you can.
- Don't forget to turn your body back in synchronization and harmony with your arms even though it is a very handsy & wristy shot.
- Your right hand is already bent over back on itself by the time the clubshaft is level & horizontal to the ground at the halfway point of the backswing.

Top Of Backswing

- Your right wrist is hinged back over on itself as far as it can go at the top of the backswing.
- Both your hands and clubface are very wide open.

Downswing

- Delay & don't start to unhinge your wrists until your hands are down to just above hip height. At this point, you unhinge as quickly as you can.

- It is a descending angle of attack into the sand, but not too steeply because you want to slice through the sand under the ball.
- Your hands are always ahead of the clubhead until just at the moment of impact when the clubhead will quickly & powerfully take the lead ahead of your hands.
- Pull your right shoulder back down and under your chin as your body turns & opens up.
- Your right hand comes down arched back on itself. In other words, it has the feeling like it is getting ready to skip a rock over some water. All the knuckles on your right hand will be pointing directly to the ground underneath.
- The clubhead comes back down from a very wide outside path slicing under the ball, towards a severe inside path. This is how you to pop the ball up high & soft.
- Uncoil your body as aggressively as you can. It is an extremely aggressive shot.
- Both of your hands are literally pulling the clubhead well to the left of the target diagonally across the target line to the inside.

Hitting Zone

- The clubface never touches the ball for a splash sand bunker shot. It slices under the ball so that the ball will come out on a soft cushion of sand. This is not a hit the ball first, then turf second type shot, it is a slice under the sand shot.
- Make sure you hold the club handle firmly & keep the clubface way open through impact.
- Aim for a very specific needle point in the sand that you want the clubhead to start sliding through. In general, the looser the sand the farther back from the ball you need to start and deeper the clubhead will go. The more compact the sand, the closer to the ball you need to start and shallower the clubhead will go.
- Keep the cut in the sand under the ball shallow and don't dig in too deep. Again, how deep or shallow and long it will be depends on the texture of the sand you are in.
- Don't focus on the ball at all. Concentrate on making sure the clubhead comes down the aimline and under the ball at the exact point you want to start in the sand & on the exact line & depth & force you think are correct.

- You need super aggressive acceleration about twice the power than for a regular swing of the same distance off the fairway. This is to make sure you create enough power to splash the sand and pop the ball up and out of the bunker successfully to where you want the ball to go.
- The swing is dominated by your right hand, especially through the sand. (Note: This is the opposite of a regular fullswing that is dominated by your left hand)
- Don't dig or push or chop the clubhead through the sand. Let the clubhead be released freely and the bounce on the bottom front edge of your clubhead to slide & splash through the sand naturally.
- Make sure you swing along the aimline parallel to your feet coming across the target line diagonally to the inside off to the left of the target.
- Keep your clubface wide open through the whole entire hitting zone & followthrough. Don't release your hands. In other words, your right hand and forearm don't rotate over your left hand & forearm as they do in a regular fullswing.
- Your right arm will straighten out and become super straight through the hitting zone.
- Your hands are more firm than for most swings, but are still free flowing & tension free.
- Your wrists unhinge forcefully at the moment of impact with the sand.
- Again, don't focus on the ball. Think about making the correct swing so that the ball will come splashing out on a soft cushion of sand. A good way to do this is to imagine that the ball is sitting on a tee and that the tee is pushed all the way down into the sand with just the cup of the tee showing. The thought is to swing through the sand below the ball and to clip through the middle of the imaginary tee underneath.
- Keep your right hand coming through as low as you can for added touch and delicacy.
- Everything in your stance stays opened up 45 degrees wide to the left of the target through the hitting zone.
- Make sure you turn your chest to the target. In other words, don't forget to fully turn through.

Followthrough

- Keep the clubface wide open facing straight up to the sky, don't release the clubhead after impact. In other words, don't rotate your right hand & forearm over your left hand & forearm like you do in a regular fullswing. Always keep the clubface wide open.
- The followthrough should be a bit longer than the backswing to make sure there is always aggressive & forward momentum through the sand.
- The clubhead will be moving so fast through the sand that by the time the ball pops up, the clubhead can actually get ahead of the ball for approximately the first 12 inches after impact.
- Get your hands to finish as high as you can to encourage the ball to come out high and soft.

Overall

- Don't swing too quickly or jerkily. It still needs to be a smooth, rhythmic & good tempo swing.
- This is the most handsy and wristy swing there is, but you still don't steer the clubhead, let the clubhead flow freely.
- Keep the swing synchronized flowing back and forth together.
- The splash sand bunker shot will only go approximately half as far as a regular fullswing shot swung at the same speed from the fairway. Therefore, double the length & power of the swing that you would use for a regular fullswing shot. You can literally aim for a spot approximately twice as far as the real target you are aiming for when splashing out of the sand.
- Make sure you keep a very steady base throughout the entire swing as this is a very aggressive swing.
- The entire swing is dominated by your right hand.
- The entire swing is a very wide outside to inside swing path. The clubhead comes down crossing the target line following your feet on a 45 degree diagonal severely to the inside.
- A lot of the clubhead speed comes from your hands and arms. It is a very wristy & handsy arm swing.

The More You Open The Clubface

- The more left than normal you need to aim.
- The shallower the clubhead will dig into the sand.
- The higher the trajectory of the shot.
- The more backspin the shot will have.
- The softer the ball will land with less roll.

The More You Close The Clubface

- The more right towards square you need to aim.
- The deeper the clubhead will dig into the sand.
- The lower the trajectory of the shot.
- The less backspin the shot will have.
- The harder the ball will land with more roll.

For More Backspin

- The less sand you take will result in more backspin because the closer the clubface gets to the ball. A thin cushion of sand will be splashed up & farther the ball will go.
- The faster & more powerful you swing through the sand will also increase the backspin.

For Less Backspin

- The more sand you take will result in less backspin because the farther down & away the clubface gets from the ball. A thick cushion of sand will be splashed up & the ball will not go as far.
- The slower & less powerful you swing through the sand will also decrease the amount of backspin.

For More Height & Softer Landing

- The farther left and more open you aim, the higher and shorter the ball will travel with a softer landing & less roll.
- The higher your hands finish in the followthrough, the higher the ball will fly and shorter distance the ball will travel with less roll.

For Less Height & Harder Landing
- The farther right towards square you aim, the lower and farther the ball will travel with a harder landing & more roll.
- The lower your hands finish in the followthrough, the lower the ball will fly and longer distance the ball will travel with more roll.

From An Upslope
- Increases the loft on your clubface. The ball will fly higher than normal, not as far, with less roll.
- Ball tends to fly a touch to the left of where you aim.
- The more severe the upslope, the more affect it will have on your shot.

From A Downslope
- Decreases the loft on your clubface. The ball will fly lower than normal, farther, with more roll.
- Ball tends to fly a touch to the right of where you aim.
- The more severe the downslope, the more affect it will have on your shot.

Ball Above Your Feet
- Your clubface needs to be almost square to dig and push the ball out. Close your clubface, don't use a wide open clubface as you would for a regular splash sand bunker shot.
- Ball tends to fly a touch to the left of where you aim and will come out very hard with much more roll than normal.

Ball Below Your Feet
- It is super important to keep your balance because it is easy to lose your balance reaching & swinging so far downwards.
- Grip up on the club to the edge of your grip handle. Make the club as long as you can make it.
- It is an even more wristy & handsy arm swing than for a normal splash sand bunker swing. In other words, it's an almost all wrists, hands & arm swing.

- Ball tends to fly a bit right and will come out like a regular shot with regular roll.

Hard Packed Sand

- Don't use your sandwedge as you normally would because it has bounce, a round front leading edge and won't get down and under the ball properly. Use a club with a sharp leading edge, such as a pitching wedge or a 9-iron.
- You'll only be able to take a little bit of sand, so remember that the ball will come out hard.
- The ball won't fly as high, will fly farther than normal with more roll on landing.

Ball Under The Lip

- Don't use your sandwedge because it has bounce, a round front leading edge and will bounce up quickly causing a mishit. Use a club with a sharp leading edge such as a pitching wedge or 9-iron to dig into the lip and drive the ball up & out.
- Ball tends to fly much higher than normal & not as far with no roll.

Ball Buried In Sand

- Stand perfectly square to the target or a touch open at the most. Setup like you would for a regular fullswing, not like you would for a splash sand bunker swing.
- Keep your clubface square to the target instead of way open like it would be for a splash sand bunker shot because the clubface won't be slicing under the ball.
- Position the ball in the exact middle of your stance.
- Keep your hands well ahead of the clubhead at address, just over your front left knee.
- You need a very steep and descending strike downwards in order to get under the ball and force that ball up & out.
- The more the ball is sunk into the sand, the farther back in your stance you need to position the ball and the more you need to square your stance and clubface so it digs in. The less the ball is

sunk into the sand, the farther forward in your stance you need to position the ball and the more you can open your stance and clubface to be like a regular splash sand bunker swing.

- Stand a touch farther away from the ball than normal.
- Bend over at the waist more than normal.
- Hinge your wrists right away as you start the backswing.
- Take a longer backswing than normal.
- Bury the clubhead into the sand as deeply as you can, thump down, drive into the sand and use more force than you might imagine.
- Take a huge sand divot using the heel of the clubhead more than the toe.
- Keep your hands & wrists very solid.
- It's a very handsy and wristy swing.
- Use lots of force, especially with your right hand.
- There will often be no followthrough as the clubhead will get stuck dead in the sand. Although, if you can, try to make a full finish to encourage the ball to get out.
- It will be a lower trajectory shot with no backspin & more roll than normal.
- Don't use a sandwedge that has bounce. Use a club with a sharp leading edge such as a pitching wedge or a 9-iron to allow the club to dig deeper into the sand.

Chipping From The Sand

- Don't try to scoop or pick the ball up with your hands. You still need to make a downward strike on the ball.
- Concentrate on keeping everything super level at address. There is no room for error with this swing in the sand.
- Ball position is not back in your stance like for a regular chipping swing, ball position is in the exact middle of your stance or just a touch back from there.
- Aim to have the clubhead make contact with the bottom quarter of the ball without digging into the sand through the hitting zone.
- Only chip from the sand when the ball is perched up on top of the sand.

- There will be more backspin than normal so the shot won't go quite as far as a regular chip shot would off the fairway.

Putting From The Sand

- Setup like you would for a regular chipping swing, don't use the putting swing.
- It's very similar to chipping from the sand, but you use your putter.
- Position the ball just a ball width forward of center to make sure you hit the ball on the upward part of the swing.
- The putterhead is still not allowed to touch the sand until impact or you get a one stroke penalty. You need to hover the putterhead above the sand.
- Hit the ball cleanly with only a slightly descending blow through the hitting zone.
- Hold the putterface pointing to the sky for as long as possible in the followthrough.
- Only putt from the sand when the sand is firm enough to let the ball roll through it. The ball also needs to be perched up on top of the sand & there can't be a front lip in the bunker.

Very Delicate Sand Shot (Under 5 Yards)

- Open your clubface so far to the right that you can almost place a glass of water on it. Make sure your stance is also wide open to the left in the opposite direction.
- Take a shallow cut of sand, much less than for a regular splash sand bunker shot.
- The shallower the cut of sand, the more backspin will be created & easier the distance of the shot will be to control.

From Fairway Bunkers (Over 50 yards)

- It's not like a greenside splash sand bunker shot at all. It's more like a regular finesse swing or fullswing.
- Position the ball a little more forward in your stance than for a regular fullswing.

- Make sure your feet are shuffled down and you make a solid foundation.
- Choke down on the club handle because your feet are sunk into the sand.
- The longer the shot, the lighter you should grip on the club handle. The shorter the shot, the more firm you should grip on the club handle.
- Finish with your hands high in the followthrough.
- From a perfect lie, hit the ball cleanly without touching any sand. It still needs to be a descending blow though impact, but don't take a divot, don't even skim the sand. Keep the clubface up and out of the sand throughout the entire hitting zone.
- From a bad lie, hit the ball first, then sand second, but still don't dig too deep. Have the ball a little farther back in your stance than normal. Don't try to scoop the ball out of the sand or your clubface will sink in and you'll end up hitting the shot heavy.
- Make sure you have enough loft on the club you choose to use to get the ball over the lip of the bunker.
- Your swing won't be as powerful in the sand, so the ball won't travel quite as far as a regular fullswing would from the fairway.
- Your restricted body turn in the sand will cause the ball to have a slight fade. Therefore, aim just a touch left.

(C)
Special Shots

(C-1) Shaping Shots

Shaping Shots

- It's a good idea to add a slight fade or draw to your shot to curve the ball away from danger on one side of the fairway or the other or to curve your ball around a dogleg.
- The less lofted the club you're using, the more the ball can be shaped. The more lofted the club you're using, the less the ball can be shaped. Therefore, a driver is the easiest club to shape a ball with & a pitching wedge or lob wedge is the hardest club to shape a ball with.

Key Points

- The alignment of your stance will get you swinging down the correct path & the clubface will be open or closed at impact causing side spin on the ball one way or the other.
- Simply align yourself in the direction you want the ball to start & aim your clubface where you want the ball to finish.
- Don't try to manipulate the clubhead with your hands during the swing, you still need to let the clubhead flow freely.
- Just make a normal swing down your aimline & keep the clubface open (fade) or closed (draw) and let the mechanics of your setup cause the ball to fade or draw.

Hitting A Fade (Slice)

<u>Course Management</u>
- The ball will start out to the left and swerve right through the air.
- The ball will travel a bit less than normal with less roll.

<u>Address</u>
- Position the ball slightly more forward than normal in your stance.
- Take a slightly narrower stance than normal.
- Open your stance. Align slightly to the left of the target.
- Open clubface slightly to the right.

<u>Overall</u>
- It's an outside-to-inside swing path. It's also a major sweeping motion swing.
- The farther to the left you align & the more you open the clubface to the right the more severe the ball will fade.
- Take a regular swing in the direction you are aimed with the clubface open.
- Don't release the clubhead though the hitting zone. In other words, don't let your right hand & forearm rotate over your left hand & forearm.

Hitting A Draw (Hook)

<u>Course Management</u>
- The ball will start out to the right and swerve left through the air.
- The ball will travel a bit farther than normal with more roll.

<u>Address</u>
- Position the ball slightly more forward than normal in your stance.
- Take a slightly wider stance than normal.
- Close your stance. Align to the right of the target.
- Close clubface slightly to the left. (or the clubface can even stay square)

Overall
- It's an inside-to-outside swing path. It's also a major sweeping motion swing.
- The farther to the right you align & the more you close the clubface to the left the more severe the ball will draw.
- Take a regular swing in the direction you are aimed with the clubface closed. (or square)
- Make sure you do a very aggressive release of the clubhead through the hitting zone. In other words, rotate your right hand & forearm over your left hand & forearm aggressively.

(C-2) Lob Shot Swing

Course Management
- You need a good lie to use a lob shot swing shot. Don't try it from a hard surface & don't try it from the deep rough unless the ball is perched up.
- The higher you want the ball to go, the more you need to open your stance & clubface.
- The ball will fly less distance with more backspin than a normal shot.

Address
- Set up like you would for a greenside splash sand bunker shot.
- Open your clubface way right of the target.
- Open your stance so that your feet, body, shoulders & eyes are all aligned way left of the target.
- Grip the club handle lighter than normal.
- Choke down on the club handle.
- Your hands are only slightly lined up just ahead of the ball.
- Ball position is still in the very middle of your stance. Don't place the ball forward in your stance trying to scoop the ball up. It's still a slightly descending blow at impact.
- Take a very narrow stance & a very tall & upright stance in order to get extra height on the ball flight.
- Weight distribution is 60% on your back right foot / 40% on your front left foot.

<u>Overall</u>

- Hinge your wrists early in the backswing. In other words, cup your right wrist back quickly.
- It's a severe outside to inside swing pattern.
- Try to slide the clubhead through the grass under the ball. But, don't try to help the ball in the air. It's still a descending blow into the back of the ball.
- Definitely hit down on the ball with a descending blow for more backspin.
- Hit off the toe of the clubhead, not the center of the clubhead in order to soften the ball on landing.
- Keep your hands and arms soft & dead weight. It's still a body-turn type shot, so don't get too handsy & wristy like you would in an actual splash sand bunker swing.
- Finish with your hands high & keep the clubface aiming at the sky for as long as possible. Don't rotate your forearms through impact. In other words, don't have your right hand & forearm rotate over your left hand & forearm.

(C-3) Driver Swing vs. Iron Swing

Course Management (Driver)

- Don't ever drive for distance, always drive for position. Choose a target where you want the ball to land and make sure you are realistic about it.
- Concentrate on having good timing, proper mechanics & unwinding & uncoiling properly. This is what causes you to hit the ball very far, not by over extending yourself and trying to smash at the ball sliding and bouncing all over the place.
- Hit your driver with the same smoothness as you would your pitching wedge.
- Remember that the driver is also just a swing, not a hit. Don't ever hit the ball, just swing through it.
- Never swing past 85% of full power, not even for the driver.

Address (Driver)

- Tee the ball up so that the top of your driver's clubface is level and lined up at the ball's equator, the middle of the golf ball.
- 60% of your weight is on your back right foot / 40% of your weight is on your front left foot. You are leaning back and away from the ball.
- Keep the clubface perfectly square.
- Have a very wide & perfectly square stance. A touch closed stance is better than a touch opened stance. A touch closed stance may even help you consistently hit the ball straighter.
- Your feet should be just outside shoulder width at the widest.

Overall (Driver)

- It's a wide, slow & stay low type sweeping swing around and behind your body. It's not as steep and upwards as a regular fullswing. Extend the butt-end of your clubshaft as far away from your right hip as you possibly can in the backswing.
- Extend your hands as far away from your head as possible in the backswing, then as far as possible towards the target in the followthrough. Making a wider and longer swing arc will help increase the distance & smoothness of the swing.
- This is the only level angle of attack into the back of the ball swing there is, not descending at impact like all the other swings. Therefore, concentrate on staying down low well through impact & sweeping the ball off the tee with the shallowest sweeping swing you can come up with.
- Think of your front left leg as the hitting zone, you swing into and through your front left leg.
- Keep your lower-body as quiet as possible throughout the entire swing.
- The tighter you wind up in the backswing, the faster your upper-body will unwind in the downswing and the farther the ball will go.
- Make sure you unwind your hips on a swivel. Don't slide your hips towards the target.
- Try your hardest to keep your whole body & head to the right behind the ball for the entire downswing.

- Make sure you literally whip your hips first, then shoulders second through the hitting zone. Don't let your shoulders unwind ahead of your arms or hips. You should feel yourself throwing your right hip first, then right shoulder second through the hitting zone and feel the need to get off your front left foot and walk towards the target in the followthrough, but don't.
- Once you get to the bottom part of this swing is the only time you can open up and give it all of your power. If you try to give all of your power in any earlier point in the swing, your swing will almost always break down and you'll end up hitting a bad shot.

Iron Shot Swing

- Short iron shots are a descending blow into the back of the ball and the divot mark will start just after the ball. The divot mark starts just after the ball because you are hitting the ball first, then turf second. Ball position is always back or in the exact middle of your stance.
- Long iron shots are a sweeping blow into the back of the ball and there is no divot mark because the ball is swept away, just the slightest bruising of the turf. It is still a slightly descending blow into the back of the ball though. Ball position is always forward in your stance.
- Always use a tee off a tee box because you are allowed & it is easier to hit the ball. Push the tee all the way into ground so just the cup of the tee is showing. Place your ball on the tee and hit your iron shot as if it was a regular shot from the fairway, forget that the tee is even there.

(C-4) Different Lie Swings

Key Points

- When you get your ball into trouble, always play safe coming out. Just get the ball back into play by choosing the safest shot possible. Don't try to make a miracle shot only to end up in a disaster. It will ruin your score & frustrate your game.

- The better a ball lies, the farther forward in your stance the ball should be positioned & more open the clubface should be.
- The worse a ball lies, the farther back in your stance the ball should be positioned & more closed the clubface should be.

From An Upslope

<u>Course Management</u>
- Ball will fly higher in the air because the upslope will add more loft to your clubface.
- Ball will travel less distance than normal.
- Ball will not roll as much on landing as normal.
- Ball will fly a touch to the left.
- The steeper the upslope, the greater the affect it will have on your shot.

<u>Address</u>
- Ball position is slightly more forward than for a normal shot. The steeper the upslope, the farther forward the ball needs to be positioned.
- Slightly open stance, but align yourself with a square clubface to the target.
- Take a slightly narrower stance than normal to give you more mobility in the swing.
- Level your shoulders & hips with the slope. Your front left shoulder will feel higher than normal.
- Spine angle is vertical to the slope on a 90 degree angle.
- Flex your knees a touch more than normal to anchor your weight in place.
- Grip down on the club handle because the ground is closer to you.
- Hands a touch farther back in stance than normal.
- 60% of your weight is on your back right foot / 40% of your weight is on your front left foot.
- The upslope will cause most of your weight to be on your back right foot, but get as much weight as you can on your front left foot.

Overall
- Don't sway back down the slope in the backswing. Keep your weight firmly anchored solidly over your back right knee.
- Focus on keeping your head super steady & not swaying backwards throughout the entire swing. You need a super steady base.
- Concentrate on turning smoothly & steadily into the ball.
- It's a sweeping blow through impact. Feel that you are swinging the clubhead up the slope with only a slight descending blow at impact.
- Keep more weight than normal on your back right foot throughout the entire swing so you can easily swing up and through impact. Keep your weight firmly anchored over your back right knee.

From A Downslope

Course Management
- Ball will fly lower in the air because the downslope will decrease loft to your clubface.
- Ball will travel more distance than normal.
- Ball will roll a lot more on landing than normal.
- Ball will fly a touch to the right.
- The steeper the downslope, the greater the affect it will have on your shot.

Address
- Ball position is slightly farther back than for a normal shot. The steeper the downslope, the farther back the ball needs to be positioned.
- Slightly closed stance, but align yourself with a square clubface to the target.
- Take a slightly wider stance than normal to give you more stability in the swing.
- Level your shoulders & hips with the slope. Your front left shoulder will feel lower than normal.
- Spine angle is vertical to the slope on a 90 degree angle.

- Flex your knees a touch more than normal to anchor your weight in place.
- Grip up on the club handle because the ground is farther away from you.
- Your hands are a touch farther ahead in your stance than normal.
- 40% of your weight is on your back right foot / 60% of your weight is on your front left foot.
- The downslope will cause most of your weight to be on your front left foot, but get as much weight as you can on your back right foot.

Overall
- Focus on keeping your head super steady & not swaying forward throughout the entire swing. You need a super steady base.
- Hinge your wrists earlier than normal for a steeply upwards backswing. Make sure you don't lean backwards into the swing, turn on a swivel.
- Concentrate on turning smoothly & steadily into the ball.
- It's a descending blow through impact. Feel that you are swinging the clubhead down the slope with a very steep descending blow at impact. Stay down with the shot following the ground & chasing the ball down the slope well into the followthrough. Don't try to lift or scoop the ball up.
- Keep your hands well ahead of the clubhead as you swing down the slope.
- Keep more weight than normal on your front left foot throughout the entire swing so you can easily swing down the slope and through impact. Keep your weight firmly anchored over your front left knee.

Ball Below Your Feet

Course Management
- You won't be able to make as powerful of a swing, so the ball will fly less distance than normal.
- Ball tends to fly just a touch to the right. The less the loft on clubface the more right the ball will go.

Address
- Grip up on the very top of the club handle because the ground is farther away from you.
- Ball position is slightly farther back than normal.
- Stand a little closer to the ball than normal to reduce overstretching.
- Bend your knees more than normal to get down to the ball.
- Widen your stance quite a bit to get down lower to the ball and for more stability.
- Keep weight distribution more on your heels than on your toes to help you from toppling forward as you swing.
- Make sure you aim slightly left of the target to compensate for the slight fade.

Overall
- Hinge your wrists earlier than normal for a steeply upwards backswing.
- It's a hands & arms dominated swing which will help you to keep your balance.
- Keep your head very steady.
- Concentrate on maintaining the same height & staying level throughout the entire swing.
- Don't overextend yourself or reach for the ball.
- Make sure you stay down through the hitting zone.

Ball Above Your Feet

Course Management
- You will be able to make an extra powerful swing so the ball will fly farther than normal with lots of roll.
- Ball will fly strongly to the left. The greater the loft on clubface the more left the ball will go.

Address
- Choke way down on the club handle because the ground is closer to you than normal.
- Stand taller and more upright than you would for a normal shot to stay up and away from the ground.

- Keep weight distribution more on your toes than on your heels to help you from toppling backwards as you swing.
- Stand a little farther back away from the ball than you normally would.
- Make sure you definitely aim slightly right of the target to compensate for the draw.

Overall
- Make a rounded backswing, more behind you than upwards. A sweeping blow.
- This is more of a full-body swing, not a hands & arms swing.
- The swing comes in more from the inside through hitting zone.
- Make sure the clubface doesn't close at impact.
- Keep your head very steady.
- Concentrate on maintaining height & staying perfectly level throughout the entire swing.

Bare Lie / Hard Surface

Course Management
- Ball will travel lower than normal with more backspin.
- Never use a club with high bounce such as your sandwedge, use a club with a sharp front edge such as a pitching wedge or a 9-iron. You don't want the clubhead to bounce off the ground, you want the clubhead to dig in.
- Ball tends to fly a touch right.

Address
- Ball position is a touch farther back than normal.
- Don't descend too much into this type of shot, but make sure it is still a descending swing.
- Don't try to scoop the ball up, make sure it is a slightly descending sweeping blow.
- Open your clubface a touch.

Overall
- Concentrate extra hard on keeping your head very steady & level throughout the entire swing.

- Keep your lower-body steadier than normal throughout the entire swing.
- Make the smoothest and most balanced hands & arms swing possible to stay perfectly balanced.

Out Of A Divot Mark

Course Management
- Ball will have a low trajectory and roll lots on landing.
- When in a loose sand divot, play it like a splash sand bunker shot.
- Ball tends to fly a bit right.

Address
- Ball position is way back in your stance. The deeper the divot, the farther back the ball needs to be positioned in your stance.
- Your hands are far forward in your stance just over your front left knee.

Overall
- It's more of a hands & arms swing than a full-body swing.
- You need a very firm hand grip to make sure the clubface won't turn at impact.
- Hinge your wrists steeply in the backswing so that the clubhead travels steeply upwards.
- Make a very steep angle of attack in the downswing and drive hard into the ball as if you are trying to drive the ball even deeper into the ground. In other words, smash the clubhead into the ground. The worse the lie & divot, the harder you need to smash into the ground.
- The followthrough will usually be super short if there is any followthrough at all.

Thick Rough / Long Grass

Course Management
- The ball will come out of the rough low and soft. Not much forward momentum and not much roll.

- Ball will have less backspin than from a normal lie.
- Ball will fly less distance than normal.
- Use a club with high bounce such as a sandwedge when the rough is deep in order to bounce up & get the ball out of there.
- When the grass is leaning towards you, you need to swing a lot harder. When the grass is leaning away from you, you don't need to swing as hard.
- The farther down in the rough the ball is sitting, the more loft you'll need at impact to get the ball up and out of there. In other words, if you are in some super long grass, don't use a 3-iron to get out of there, you might need to use a 5-iron or 9-iron instead.
- When you are in a super bad lie and the long grass is leaning against you, you'll need to use the splash sand bunker shot in order to get the ball up and out of there successfully.
- Ball tends to fly a touch to the left.

Address
- Ball position is in the middle of your stance for regular rough shots. The worse the lie & longer the grass, the farther back the ball needs to be positioned in your stance.
- Take a narrower stance than normal.
- Stand a bit taller than normal.
- Raise your hands a touch higher than normal.
- Choke down on the club handle.
- Keep a very firm grip on the club handle.
- 50% of your weight is on your back right foot / 50% of your weight is on your front left foot.
- Open your stance a touch to the left to encourage your hips to turn.
- Hover the clubhead up at the ball's equator so you won't get snagged in the backswing.
- Open your clubface a touch because the long grass tends to wrap itself around the blade and close the clubface a touch at impact.

Overall
- Hinge your wrists steeply in the backswing.
- Swing your hands up higher in the backswing than normal.
- You need a very steep descending strike of the clubhead into the back of the ball.

- Strike the ball hard, punch down and through aggressively, powerfully.
- You still need a clean strike of the ball, don't hit too far behind the ball. It's a ball first, then turf second shot. (Note: It is not a turf first, then ball second shot)
- It's more of a hands & arms dominated swing.
- There will usually be a super short followthrough.

The Ball Partially Submerged In Water Swing

Course Management
- Take off your shoes and socks.
- Treat it like a splash sand bunker shot.

Overall
- Accelerate & swing like mad through impact. It's tougher than sand, so swing at least 50% harder than you would for a splash sand bunker shot. This can be more than 300% harder than you would swing for a regular fullswing shot of the same distance off the fairway.
- The deeper the ball is in the water, the harder you'll need to swing.
- Ball position is well forward in your stance when the ball is near the top of the water. Ball position is in the very middle of your stance when the ball is submerged all the way under the water.

(D)
Putting Swing

(D-1) Putting Grip

Grip Pressure

- The putting grip is a much different grip than the main fundamental fullswing grip.
- It's an extremely sensitive, soft, comfortable, relaxed, free and super loose hand grip.
- It's the lightest grip you can possibly make.
- The club handle is literally about to fall out of your hands.
- You want the softest & lightest grip that you can possibly make to help you feel the distance and speed of your putts better.

The Steps

- Place your left hand on the putter handle with your thumb pointing straight down the middle of the grip handle. Then, wrap your three lowest fingers around the putter handle. Keep your left forefinger off the putter handle for a moment.
- Place your right hand on the putter handle with your right thumb on top of your left thumb pointing straight down the middle of the grip handle also. Then, wrap your three lowest fingers around the putter handle.
- Extend the forefinger on your right hand all the way down the right side of the grip handle to help you control the putter & to stop both wrists from hinging.
- Place the forefinger of your left hand on top of these four fingers.
- Squeeze both hands together as close and snug as possible.
- Your hands are perfectly parallel to each other & square to the putterface. The crease between your thumb and forefinger on

73

both hands will create two lines that run parallel to each other. Right hand line is pointing to approximately your right ear & left hand line is pointing approximately to your left ear.

- The putting grip is held more in your palm, not in the fingers like it is in the fullswing grip.
- The club handle runs up the exact middle of your left palm & square with your left forearm.
- The club handle runs up the middle of the lower half of your right palm. It isn't up the exact middle of your palm like it is for your left hand.

(D-2) Address

Club & Ball
- Hover the putterhead just above the ground to encourage a smooth takeaway.
- Bottom of putterface is level with the ground.
- Ball position is forward in your stance approximately halfway between dead center and your front left foot. You want the ball forward in your stance in order to strike the ball on the upswing.
- Clubface is perfectly square.

Hands
- Your hands are super soft, relaxed & basically asleep. You are almost about to drop the club handle out of your hands.
- Both of your hands are directly below your shoulders.
- Both of your hands point directly down at the ground 90 degrees to squeeze the shot.
- Both of your hands are level with the puttershaft so the grip handle is not trying to pry itself out.

Arms
- Both arms are simply dead weight hanging down from your shoulders. They are loose & comfortable a touch up from vertical.
- Both arms feel like two lengthy thick rubber bands.

- Bottom half of both arms bend up slightly up at the elbows.
- Both elbows are tucked in close to your hips.
- Both forearms are square & parallel to your aimline & both forearms are parallel to the perfectly square clubface.

Shoulders

- Perfectly square and parallel to the aimline.
- Very relaxed & tension free.

Head

- Head is dead steady like a concrete pillar.
- Both eyes are parallel to the aimline & directly over the aimline.
- Your left eye needs to be directly over the ball.

Back

- Back solid & straight as a board, yet comfortable & at ease.
- Stand as tall & erect as you can.
- Butt is pushed out slightly.
- Pull your stomach muscles in & tighten your abdominal muscles.
- Bend over from your hips just enough so that when you bring your palms together in front of you is the exact position where your hands need to be to make the grip on your putter handle.

Legs

- Knees slightly bent & relaxed, but solid as a concrete foundation.
- Both legs are locked in place without feeling uncomfortable.
- Flex all the muscles down both your legs in order to stay balanced and to keep a super solid base.

Feet

- The inside of both your feet are shoulder width apart.
- Both feet are square and parallel to the aimline.
- 60% of your weight is on your heels / 40% of your weight is on your toes.

- 60% of your weight is on your back right foot / 40% of your weight is on your front left foot.

Overall

- Extremely comfortable and relaxed.
- No tension anywhere.
- Your body is locked in place. (Feet, legs, hips, back, neck, head)
- Swinging parts are as loose and free as can be. (Club, hands, arms & shoulders)
- The flow lines running through your shoulders, forearms, hips, knees, feet, and eyes are all perfectly parallel to your aimline.

(D-3) Backswing

Club & Ball

- Sweep the putterhead straight back on a very gentle and gradual upward curve.
- The longer the swing, the farther upwards and more to the inside the putterhead will naturally flow.
- Keep the clubface perfectly square to both your hands & forearms.
- For short putts, bring the putterhead straight back down the aimline.
- For longer putts, you need to bring the putterhead back down the aimline, but it will be curving slightly to the inside.

Hands

- Your hands are still asleep & super soft.
- Your wrists are locked in place. They don't hinge even the slightest bit.
- Don't pull the putterhead upwards & inside with your hands, let the putterhead naturally flow upwards & inside on its own gradual arc & curve.

Arms

- Don't use the muscles in your arms to pull the putterhead backwards.
- Flow back with the turning motion of your shoulders & upper-back, not your arms.

Shoulders

- Rock your shoulders back working in harmony with the swinging clubhead, hands & arms.

Head

- Keep your eyes looking straight down at the ball.
- Head stays dead still in place.

Overall

- A synchronized & smooth one-piece takeaway. Your shoulders, arms, hands & putterhead all move away together at the exact same time.
- Keep the putterhead very steady.
- Keep the putterhead relatively close to the ground even as it slightly curves upwards.
- Keep the backswing short because the less you bring the putterhead back, the less room there is to make an error. But, also make sure the backswing is long enough to make sure you will have an unhurried & positive downswing.
- Match the backswing length to the distance you want the ball to roll.

(D-4) Top Of Backswing

Club & Ball

- Make sure the clubface is still perfectly square to both your hands & forearms.

Hands

- The putterhead will lag behind your hands for a split second while it slowly and softly stops to change direction.
- There is only a very slight bend of your wrists as you change direction from backswing to downswing.
- The lag will heighten the sensation in your wrists for a smoother acceleration forwards.

(D-5) Downswing

Club & Ball

- Make sure the clubface is still perfectly square to both your hands & forearms.
- For short putts, let the putterhead flow straight down the aimline.
- For longer putts, you need to let the putterhead flow down naturally on the same slight curve it went back on.

Hands

- Your hands are dead quiet, but will add just a touch of gentle force that will heighten the sensation & forward momentum of the swinging putterhead.

(D-6) Hitting Zone

Club & Ball

- The putterhead must still be accelerating at impact, free releasing, not decelerating, even for the shortest putts.
- Need a smooth, deliberate & solid strike at impact with exactly the same tempo & rhythm every single time.
- Make sure the clubface is perfectly square to your target at impact. The clubface is still also perfectly square to both your hands and forearms.

- Always hit the ball off the sweetspot on the putterface. In other words, hit the ball in the exact middle of the putterface for 100% distance consistency.
- The putterface should contact the ball just after the bottom of your swing arc so it is a slightly upwards stroke giving the ball a touch of topspin and a smooth roll.
- The bottom of your putterhead comes very close to the ground, but it does not touch or scrape the ground. There is no contact with the ground whatsoever.
- Don't try to hit the ball, always stroke through the ball. It's a swing, not a hit.

Hands

- Keep the putterface very stable through impact, but don't tighten your hands. Your hands are still asleep & very soft. They haven't tightened a bit.
- Your wrists are soft & still locked in place. Don't flick your wrists forward through impact, they are still asleep as well.
- Your hands are now in the same position that they were in at address, directly below your shoulders & directly above the putterhead. Your hands are not ahead or behind the putterhead through impact. In other words, the puttershaft is pointing straight down towards the ground on a 90 degree angle at impact.

Arms

- Elbows are now in the same position they were in at address. Both elbows are parallel to the aimline & level to the ground.
- Forearms are still square and in the same position they were at address.
- Arms still feel like two lengthy thick rubber bands. Don't pull through the hitting zone with your arms, let your arms flow.

Overall

- Every body part & every club part is now back in the exact same position they were in at address.

- Don't hit the ball, it's just a smooth swing and the ball gets in the way of the swinging putterhead.
- Concentrate & focus on the purest swing you can come up with.

(D-7) Followthrough

Club & Ball
- The putterhead finishes a bit higher than it went back in the backswing.
- Make sure the clubface is still perfectly square to both your hands and forearms.
- For short putts, let the putterhead continue to flow straight down the aimline.
- For longer putts, you need to let the putterhead flow slightly to the inside.

Hands
- Your wrists don't hinge after impact at all.
- Your hands don't release the putterhead after impact. In other words, your right hand & forearm don't rotate over your left hand & forearm like they do in a regular fullswing.

Head
- Keep your eyes looking straight down at the ground where the ball was for at least one second after impact.
- Your head hasn't moved a touch up or down, left or right. It is dead still in the exact same place it was at address.

Overall
- Hold the finish until you feel the touch of the putt you just made.

(D-8) Overall

Club & Ball

- Butt-end of your putter points directly to the middle of your chest for the entire swing.
- It is paramount to keep the putterface square & stable throughout the entire swing. There is never any face rotation. Face angle is much more important than the path of the putterhead for keeping the ball rolling straight. That said, it is still important to keep the putterface on the correct path.
- Hitting the ball out of the sweetspot on your putterface will increase your ability to judge distances. In other words, hit out of the dead center of your putterface every single time.
- The swing arc for the putting swing is saucer shaped. A gradual upward curve in the backswing, a gradual downward curve in the downswing, followed by a gradual upward curve again in the followthrough.
- For short putts, it is an exact straight line back, down straight and through straight. Square-to-square-to-square.
- For longer putts, your putterface will curve slightly inside on the backswing, down towards square & just makes it to square at impact, then slightly back inside again on the followthrough. A slight inside-to-square-to-inside swinging path.
- You only need a gentle acceleration of the putterhead to create a stable & square stroke.
- Swing your putterhead back and forth at the exact same tempo for every single putt. For longer putts, just make a longer backswing, don't swing any harder.
- Slow, even pace, easy, very smooth, gentle acceleration, no sudden change in speed, no jerkiness, don't force it, let it happen, natural, touch, delicacy, good rhythm, don't hurry it, tension free, relaxed & just let your putterhead flow.

Hands

- Don't use any power from your fingers, wrists or hand muscles. They are fully asleep with no tension for the entire swing.

- Grip pressure is so light that the club is always just about to fall from your hands for the entire swing.
- Grip pressure is very light and unchanging for the entire swing.
- Both hands need to work as one unit, not independent of each other. In other words, both hands feel as one.
- Both hands keep the clubface extremely steady and square.
- Wrists remain solid, locked in place & never hinge for the entire swing. There is a slight bend of your wrists in the transition from backswing to downswing, but there is never an actual hinge.

Arms

- Both arms are simply connected to the putter to form a long pendulum for this pure pendulum putting swing that swings at the exact same tempo & rhythm every single time.
- Don't use any power from your forearm muscles.
- Forearms stay square & locked in place for the entire swing, don't release them. In other words, your right hand and forearm doesn't rotate over your left hand & forearm.
- Angle of your elbows remains the same for the entire swing.
- Keep both elbows as close to your hips as they can be. But, keep them comfortable and free at the same time.

Shoulders

- Only a little bit of power comes from your shoulders. Most of the power for the putting swing comes from your upper-back & abdominal muscles.
- Shoulders purpose is mostly to swing your arms on a pendulum.
- Shoulders only move back and forth by going up and down, not turning or coiling around your spine and rotating like they do in a regular fullswing.
- The most important part of your body to keep parallel and online for the entire swing are your shoulders.

Head

- You are looking straight down at the ball for the entire swing. But, don't concentrate on hitting the ball, only concentrate &

focus on making a super smooth stroke. Use the ball as a target to aim for, but don't think about hitting it, think about the smooth swing.

- Keep your head steady as a rock for the entire swing. Your head never moves a touch up or down, left or right. It's a concrete pillar.

Back

- The putting swing is controlled mostly by your upper-back & abdominal muscles. Concentrate on your upper-back & abdominal muscles when making the swing, don't concentrate or focus on the putterface.
- Tighten your abdominal muscles throughout the entire swing for a more solid foundation & smoother stroke.
- Don't turn or rotate your upper-body or back throughout the entire swing. Your upper-body & back stay square to the aimline.
- Don't rotate your hips throughout the entire swing. Your hips stay square to the aimline and don't move at all. Your hips are as steady as concrete pillars.
- The hinge of the putting swing is in the middle of your upper-body.

Legs

- There is no leg movement or weight shifting.
- Both legs are as steady as concrete pillars.

Feet

- Your weight doesn't sway back and forth like it does in a regular fullswing.
- 60% of your weight is on your heels / 40% of your weight is on your toes for the entire swing.
- 40% of your weight is on your back right foot / 60% of your weight is on your front left foot for the entire swing.

Overall

- Your whole body must be dead still. There is no body motion or swaying at all. Concentrate on keeping dead still throughout the entire swing, especially your head and hips.
- The only moving part on this putting swing is the pendulum. The club, hands, arms & shoulders form one triangle machine piece that stays in the exact same triangle shape for the entire swing. This pendulum moves smoothly back and forth all together in a one-piece motion. In other words, you are essentially a standing grandfather clock.
- Again, keep this putting triangle shape for the entire swing. In other words, your elbow and wrist angles don't change throughout the entire swing. Your hands & forearms don't rotate and your hands always stay under your shoulders.
- The swinging pendulum back and forth is a gentle, constant, rhythmic & harmonic motion.
- Don't try to control the distance of the putt with any of your hand or arm muscles. It's the length of your swing that will control the distance the ball rolls.
- The putterhead is swinging in rhythm with your arms, hands & wrists, but no power comes from your arms, hands or wrists.
- Control the amount of acceleration in your stroke from your upper-back & abdominal muscles.
- It's a gentle swinging motion back and through, just let it flow.
- Remember not to hit your putts. You simply need to have a smooth flowing & rhythmic putting stroke. You are not trying to hit the ball. You are trying to make the most perfect putting swing you can come up with. The ball just gets in the way of the swing.

(E)
Putting Course Management

(E-1) Reading The Green

Key Points

- Make sure you are reading the correct break. There are many lines to think & worry about.
- You need to aim your putterface and set everything up in your putting stance approximately 3 times higher than where you will actually see the ball rolling.
- The visual break (ball track) is approximately 1/3 of the true break (aimline). You need to know this in order to know where to precisely aim your putterface & align your stance. If you don't know this, you'll always be under reading the amount of break on your putts and you'll be missing most of your putts low of the hole because of this.
- Almost every single putt breaks at least a little bit.
- Use your own judgment because no two people perceive the same putt in exactly the same way.
- When unsure of the break, always allow for more break than you think. Take the high road, not the low road, because by far, the most common place you'll likely miss your putt is on the low side of the hole.

True Break (Aimline)

- The true break is where you aim your putterface. But, the true break (aimline) is approximately 3 times higher than the visual break (ball track) where you actually see the ball rolling.

Therefore, make sure you are always aiming approximately 3 times higher than where the ball will actually roll.

- Line everything up in your stance parallel to the true break line. (aimline)
- This is where you putt. This is where you stroke the ball towards, but the ball immediately starts to follow the visual break line (ball track) approximately 1/3 of where you are aiming.

Visual Break (Ball Track)

- Visual break (ball track) is where you actually see the ball rolling.
- Visual break is approximately 1/3 of the true break (aimline).
- This is the line you visualize the ball rolling from your putterface to the hole. It is the highest point the ball actually reaches.
- Do not aim putts along this line though or you'll always miss the hole on the low side.
- Where you see your ball rolling is not where you aim your putterface. You aim your putterface approximately 3 times higher than this.

Ball Track (Visual Break)

- Ball track (visual break) is the entire path that your ball rolls on.
- Ball track is determined by speed. How fast or slow the ball is rolling will change the ball track it follows.
- You can set up a putt along the same aimline & hit various putts at different speeds and you'll end up with many different ball tracks.

Aimline (True Break)

- Aimline (true break) is where your clubface is aiming. It is the direction you intend the putt to start on. Although, it is approximately 3 times higher than where the ball actually rolls.
- Set everything up in your stance along the aimline (true break). Feet, hips, knees, shoulders, elbows, forearms & eyes all need to be running on a line parallel to your aimline.
- When you stroke the putterface back and forth it is along this aimline as well.

86

- You stroke the ball down this line and as soon as you do, the ball follows the visual break line (ball track) which is approximately 1/3 of what you just read.
- Your putt will never stay on the line you start it on.
- True break is invisible to see. But, you always need to aim down this a true break (aimline). This is where you want your putt to start, but you'll never see your putt actually roll there. (Unless the putt is perfectly straight)
- There is more than one aimline possible. If you roll the ball at different speeds, each roll will need a different aimline in order to get the ball into the hole.

Flow Lines

- Flow lines are all parallel to your true break line (aimline) and go through your feet, knees, hips, forearms, shoulders, head & eyes.

(E-2) What Affects The Break

Speed

- How fast a ball is putted will affect how much it will break.
- The faster a ball rolls, the less it will break.
- The slower a ball rolls, the more it will break.
- Finding the correct speed is much more important than finding the correct line of a putt. But, don't think of putting as finding the correct speed. Think of putting as a distance to aim for. Your subconscious mind will figure out the speed for you. Putting is all about distance.

The Last 10% Of Your Putt

- The last 10% of every putt affects your putt the most because this is when the ball is rolling at its slowest.
- Since the last 10% of your putt will be traveling the slowest, this is what area you need to worry about the most.

Wind
- Breezy days will not affect your putts at all.
- The windier it is, the more it will affect your putting.
- The faster the greens are, the more affect wind will have on your putting. The slower the greens are, the less affect wind will have on your putting.
- A crosswind blowing across the green will make you to have to add a little more break or take away from the break that is truly there.
- A tailwind will speed up the putt.
- A headwind will slow down the putt.

Grain Direction
- The direction the grain grows will only affect your putting a touch.
- Putting with the grain will speed up your putt.
- Putting against the grain will slow down your putt.
- Putting against a crossways grain will keep the putting speed the same.

Other Stuff Affecting Break
- All the imperfections on a green like footprints, cleat marks & pitch marks get worse as the day goes on.
- The closer a green is mown, the faster it is. The longer a green is mown, the slower it is.
- The drier a green is, the faster it is. The wetter a green is, the slower it is.

Treat Every Putt As A Straight Putt
- Decide on what line you want the ball to start out on and then let the break and ball roll the way it does. Always putt out in a straight line in your mind's eye.

Always Miss Your Putts 18 Inches Past The Hole

- It doesn't matter if you are putting uphill or downhill, always aim to miss the hole by 18 inches is the perfect length to miss a putt by.

- Although, if you putt the ball more than 24 inches past the hole it never any good, and a putt that is short of the hole will always miss 100% of the time. In other words, putting a ball too far past the hole is incorrect & putting a ball too short of the hole is not supposed to ever happen if you can help it. A putt that goes past the hole at least has a chance to go in.

- Having a good solid putting stroke that moves the ball 18 inches past the hole makes sure the ball will also hold its line as it approaches the hole. This is the last 10% of your putt where all sorts of subtle breaks can knock your ball offline.

Keep Putterface Square

- Keeping the putterface square to your target is much more important than your swinging putterhead path.

Concentrate On Distance Not Aimline

- Concentrating on the distance of the putt is much more important than how you are lined up once you are finally lined up & getting ready to putt. This is because once you are lined up, you should be lined up correctly anyways. Being lined up correctly is a given.

- Making sure you are always lined up correctly is a very important fundamental. As the saying goes "the better you aim, the better you'll putt". But, you need to be concentrating on distance because putting down the aimline is the exact same every single time & distance is the major challenge that always varies.

- Firstly, always setup your aim perfectly.

- Secondly, always keep your putterface square throughout the entire swing.

- Thirdly, focus 100% of your energy and focus on judging the distance of the putt only.

Putting On Slopes Affects Distance Perception

- Uphill putts – (10 foot measured off putt) – The hole will be approximately 10 feet from your eyes. The distance will appear shorter to you than it really is. Therefore, you'll tend to leave these putts short. You need to hit these putts with more energy than you think.
- Level putts – (10 foot measured off putt) – The hole will be approximately 11 feet from your eyes. The distance will appear to you to be normal. Therefore, you'll tend to putt these putts perfectly. You just hit these putts with regular energy.
- Downhill putts – (10 foot measured off putt) – The hole will be approximately 12 feet from your eyes. The distance will appear to you longer than it really is. Therefore, you'll tend to hit these putts long. You need to be more delicate and hit these putts with less energy than you think.

The 16 Foot Circle Around The Hole

- Measure 8 feet out from the hole in every direction becomes a 16 foot wide circle with the hole being in the dead center. This is where you want all your long lag putts to end up. This is your target, this is your goal.
- The goal in putting is not to make a lot of 1 putts. It is to never 3 putt and sometimes 1 putt. You need to get all your long lag putts into that 16 foot circle so that you have a good chance to 2 putt.
- The reason you usually 3 putt is not because you didn't make your 2nd putt, but because you didn't get your 1st putt close enough.
- Good distance judgment is essential for long lag putts so you can get the ball in close enough to finish with your 2nd putt. In other words, the closer to the hole you make your 1st putt, the greater chance you leave yourself to make your 2nd putt & 2 putting is what good golf strategy is all about.

Stop 3 Putting!

- Becoming very good at lagging long putts in from long distances will save you more strokes than trying to become very good at making 1st putts from short distances. That said, short putts are still very important too.

Putting From Off The Green

- If the grass surface is flat and hard enough to putt over, choosing to putt can often be an easier shot than trying to chip.

Putting On Dry vs. Wet Greens

- The less moisture on a green, the faster it will be.
- The more moisture on a green, the slower it will be.
- Greens are generally more wet after it has rained, on cold days & early in the morning.
- Greens are generally more dry when it hasn't rained, on hot days & in the middle of the daytime.

Putting On Hot vs. Cold Days

- The hotter it is, the faster the green will be.
- The colder it is, the slower the green will be.

Putting On Closely vs. Highly Mown Greens

- The shorter the green is mowed, the faster the green will be.
- The longer the green is mowed, the slower the green will be.

(E-3) Different Types Of Putts

Fast Rolling Putts

- Decreases the break. Fast rolling putts don't break as much. This is because the faster a ball is rolling gravity has less time to pull the ball down.

Slow Rolling Putts
- Increases the break. Slow rolling putts break more. This is because the slower a ball is rolling gravity has more time to pull the ball down.

Uphill Putts
- Hit uphill putts more solid & aggressively.
- Tendency is to leave uphill putts short.
- It's much more difficult to roll an uphill putt too far past the hole.
- Decreases break. Uphill putts don't break as much because the ball will be travelling faster.

Downhill Putts
- Hit downhill putts more sensitive & delicately.
- Tendency is to hit downhill putts too far.
- It's much more likely that you'll roll a downhill putt too far past the hole.
- Increases break. Downhill putts break more because the ball will be travelling slower.

Fast Greens
- The faster a green is will increase the break. The ball will break more because the lighter you need to hit the ball and therefore slower the ball will be rolling.

Slow Greens
- The slower a green is will decrease the break. The ball will break less because the harder you need to hit the ball and therefore faster the ball will be rolling.

Uphill Putts With Lots Of Break
- You'll tend to over read the break and miss these putts short & high of the hole.

- Putt the ball harder than you think & allow for less break than you think.

Downhill Putts With Lots Of Break

- You'll tend to under read the break and hit these putts way too far & low of the hole.
- Putt the ball lighter than you think & allow for more break than you think.

Severe Downhill Putts

- Grip way down on the putter grip.
- You can even hit off the toe of the putterface instead of the middle of putterface to lessen the blow.
- These putts are extremely delicate & in serious danger of rolling way past the hole.

Short Putts (Less Than 6 feet)

- Keeping the putt straight & online is your only focus, not the distance of the putt. These putts are all about 100% direction only.
- It is a straight back, straight forward putter path.
- Pretend that the hole is covered and always aim to stroke the ball 18 inches past the hole.
- Never lag the putt in there just enough to fall into the hole. A firm & solid strike is always necessary.
- The slower a ball is rolling as it approaches the hole, the more chance it will be deflected away. The faster a ball is rolling as it approaches the hole, the less chance it will be deflected away.
- You make a solid putt to avoid many of the slight imperfections & subtle slopes or variations on the green around the hole that could cause your ball to go offline.
- You also want to hit the ball solidly to stop the ball from breaking left or right.
- Don't allow for as much break on a short putt as you would for a longer putt.

- Treat most short putts as straight putts unless there is an obvious large break visible.
- You never want to miss these putts short. If you're going to miss the putt, you need to miss long.
- Don't guide the putterhead or jab or pop at the ball. A regular free flowing pendulum putting swing is still necessary to release the putterhead freely and squarely.
- Don't get nervous and stiffen up because of the pressure of a short putt. Stay relaxed, tension free, calm down, stay loose, take a deep breath.
- Aim at a single point, a smaller detail within the hole, not just the whole hole. Narrow your shot down to a very specific target, a slight imperfection on the rim of the cup, or a spot on the green somewhere that you want to be lined up with. Always aim for the bulls-eye like shooting a gun, don't just aim off in the distance, even if it's a short distance.

Medium Putts (7 To 30 Feet)

- You still pretend that the hole is covered and aim to have the ball finish 18 inches past the hole.
- You are still not far enough away to lag the putt in.
- Distance of the putt is much more important now than staying on a straight line.
- It's a slight inside-to-square-to-inside putter path.

Long Putts (Over 30 Feet)

- Do not aim to strike the ball 18 inches past the hole anymore. This is a long lag putt. You aim to stroke the ball just enough so that the ball will drop into the hole just as the ball stops rolling.
- Your goal is to get your putt within the 16 foot circle around the hole. (Note: You still need to aim for the dead center of that circle though, the hole)
- Use the length of backswing, not the speed of your stroke to control the distance.
- A slower, gentler and longer stroke is needed.

- It's a slight inside-to-square-to-inside putter path.
- Distance of the putt is way more important than staying on a straight line.

(E-4) Putting Is A Mental Art Form

Positive Thinking

- You need to truly believe that you will make each putt. You need to be positive that the ball is going to go in.
- Having a positive & good attitude towards your putt will give you a confidence boost and keep your mind relaxed and calm.
- Push all negative & distracting thoughts away & never be nervous or afraid of a putt you are about to make.
- Never think that the ball is going to miss. Always think that the ball is going to go in the hole, in your mind's eye.
- It's mind over matter. It's up to you how you think. You are the one in control. You choose your perspective on things.
- Always place positive thoughts in your mind. Speak to yourself confidently. "I am a good putter" "I am a really good putter" "I am one of the best putters there is" "This is going to be one of the most beautiful and smoothest strokes ever" "This one is going to go straight in the hole!" Having lots of positive & confident thoughts will literally help you putt better.
- Being positive helps you clear your mind, concentrate & focus on the perfect stroke which improves your feel, rhythm & touch.
- If you don't believe you will make the putt, you likely won't. Self-doubt is one of the most destructive thoughts you can have.
- Think about where you want the ball to go, not where it is going to miss. What you are thinking about is much more likely what will happen.
- Having a positive attitude and trusting yourself will improve your putting far more than you may realize.

The Hole Is Almost 3 Balls Wide

- A golf hole is 4.25 inches wide. A golf ball is 1.68 inches in diameter.
- Always remember that the hole is almost 3 balls wide. Stay positive. You can do it!

Stay Relaxed

- Try very hard not to feel any pressure.
- Try very hard not to be nervous.
- Slow down & don't be so anxious & fidgety.
- Take some deep breathes, breathe.
- Stay extremely calm.
- Being relaxed will increase the smoothness & rhythm of your putts.
- Never feel the pressure to hurry up by your peers or by a group behind you, take your time & relax.
- Always make your putts slowly & patiently.

Visualize The Putt

- Visualize putting the ball into the back of the hole.
- Putting is an art, use your imagination, dream, creativity, and paint a pretty picture of the perfect putt in your mind's eye.
- Watch the ball rolling down the perfect ball track & into the hole before you decide to putt the ball for real.
- Think smoothly, gently, rhythmic, wonderful & amazing.

Get In The Zone

- Focus, narrow in, get in the zone, concentrate & focus on the task at hand.
- Don't let anything, anybody, or any thought distract you.
- You need to be 100% focused on your objective.
- Get ready for you next shot by blocking everything out.
- Give it your all! Want it. How badly do you really want it? Raise your level of expectation & elevate your level of performance to the next level.

- Don't be defensive or scared, go for it!

It's All In Your Mind
- Your mind is what controls your body parts, your body parts is what controls the putter, your putter is what controls the ball's roll. It all starts with your mind. Your mind is the key to great putting.
- Your mind is what reads the greens, sets up the aimline, makes a square putterface & determines the distance of the putt. Your mind is what focuses, stays positive, keeps things relaxed & smooth. Your mind is the start of everything.

Keep It Simple
- The simpler it is, the simpler it is to replicate.
- The simpler it is, the more confidence you'll have to do it.
- Take the complex and break it down into the simple.
- Simpler is always better.

Have A Carefree Attitude
- Definitely think positively for the ball to go into the hole, but then whatever happens, you just need to let happen.
- Be the most easygoing, relaxed & worry-free person on the course.
- You always need to think positively that the ball will go into the hole, but whether or not it actually goes in, you don't care!
- Your next miss is always right around the corner.
- Let fate take its course.
- Be willing to accept all your misses or you'll be setting yourself up for disappointment. Disappointment is a negative & thinking negatively will ultimately ruin your score.

After Thoughts
- You will be one smart & wise person to leave disappointment and frustration out of your golf game.
- Never worry about whether the ball goes in the hole or not.

- Sometimes you win, sometimes you lose, it's all good. Just keep trying your best! Life isn't perfect.
- Accept adversity and move on whether it was a miss, mistake or a mishit. It's over now. Never look back, it's always time to move on!

(F)
Swinging Thought Processes

(F-1) Fullswing & Finesse Swing Routine

Spot Mark Every Shot

- Spot marking is choosing a point or smaller target online with the real target. The real target might be 250 yards away for example, but the spot mark will only be 10 to 20 yards ahead of you.
- Only focus and aim on this closer target will increase your chances of hitting the ball straight & to where you want the ball to go in the distance. This is better than aiming for the real target way off in the distance that will not be as accurate as aiming for something so close & online, a spot mark.

Thought Process For Each Shot

- Start planning your next shot well before it's your turn to hit so you don't slow anyone down, you are never rushing & you can always take it easy.
- Always start your strategy at the green and work your way back from there. Think ahead.
- Remember that low shots with roll are more accurate to hit than high shots with no roll right to the flag. So, whenever you can, always use a low trajectory shot to get the ball rolling to the target. You don't always have to fly the ball into the flag.
- Remember how you tend to hit the ball. Most people tend to have some sort of slice or fade on the ball. Take that into consideration when you aim.

- Always avoid out-of-bounds. Avoid taking risks will put your mind at ease. Always aim towards a safe area & well away from any trouble. (water, very long grass, trees, bushes, sand traps, out-of-bounds etc.)

Getting Ready
- Where can you leave the ball for the easiest next shot?
- Hit to flat areas or dips in the ground. Avoid hitting your ball to humps in the terrain because it is unpredictable how the ball will bounce off a hump.
- Access the lie for the type of shot required.
- What is the distance to the target?
- Check the flag position. Is it in the front, middle or back of the green? Will you need to add, subtract or keep the distance measurement the same? When you are in between yardage, always take the next club up and swing a little easier, smoother. Never club down and try to hit the ball harder than your speed limit of 85% of full power.
- What direction is the wind blowing? How strong? Look at the clouds, tree tops, leaves etc.
- Are you hitting up a hill or down a hill or over even ground?
- How is the green sloped? Towards you, away from you, left or right or flat?
- Where can the ball safely miss the target? Left, right, long or short?

Planning For The Shot
- Stand two steps behind the ball.
- Take a very deep breath and block everything out.
- Get into it. Concentrate. Don't be lazy. Pay attention & focus on what your objective is.
- Make the perfect grip while checking for a spot mark. Always spot mark.
- Visualize your perfect shot flying over the spot mark. See it & feel it in your mind's eye. Watch the ball land, watch the ball go all the way from start to finish. Imagine the ball flowing perfectly

to the target. Know & feel what your perfect swing is going to look like before you try and make it.

- Do a couple practice swings. Feel the looseness, freeness, rhythm & tempo. Feel your hands, feel the clubhead, feel the turning motion of your body. Visualize yourself swinging to hit the perfect shot you just visualized.

Pre-Shot Routine

- Walk into your stance with your front left foot & left hand on the clubhandle and the clubface square to your spot mark and target. It is like aiming a gun, you need to be precise with dead on aim.
- Walk into your stance focusing on the spot mark to ball. Don't take your eyes off this line.
- Bend from the waist until the clubhead just touches the ground.
- Build your stance around this clubface position.
- Consciously stand straight up tall to make sure you aren't slouching so your swing will be made at the same height and angles every single time.
- Rock your shoulders gently back and forth to make sure you are on the correct line.
- Waggle #1 – Shake everything to release tension.
- Waggle #2 – Take the clubhead straight back to make sure it is online.
- Have one last look at the target, then back to the spot mark, then back to the ball. Make sure you see the line. Make sure your shoulders are on the correct line, not too open and not too closed, rocking them back and forth.

The Ritual

- Waggle #3 – Get all tension away from your body one last time. Then gently rest your clubhead down like it's resting on an eggshell just behind the ball.
- Loosen your hand grip by 5% is your trigger that it's time to start the takeaway.

- Only concentrate on feeling your hands for the rest of the swing now. Concentrating on your hands and feeling them throughout the swing will result in a better rhythmic & smoother swing.
- Pull back, a one-piece take-away, slowly and smoothly, un-rushed.
- Start without any tension whatsoever. It should feel as if someone else or some mysterious force is helping you to pull the clubhead away.
- Make the most perfect & eloquent swing possible.

Finishing The Shot

- Stay in your perfectly balanced followthrough stance for at least three seconds. It's like you are posing for a photograph.
- Any frustration or happiness can be released for a few seconds, then get back to neutral emotions right away.
- Walk out of the past and into the present. Prepare for the future with emotionally neutral thinking. Relax, laugh, have fun again, the shot is over.
- Spot mark to a tree or pole or some object and remember this location so it will be easier to find your ball for the next shot. Less stress, less anxiety, less time wasted trying to locate your ball once you get up there.

(F-2) Chipping Swing Routine

Always Chip If You Can!

- The chip shot has a lower trajectory than a flop shop and is less affected by the wind.
- The chip shot has less backspin and is more accurate to bounce and run up to the flag than a flop shot is to carry to the flag.
- Even a 125 yard bump and run shot with a 5-iron is similar to a chip shot and as long as nothing is in the way and you can roll it right up to the green is a much more accurate shot to take than trying to make a flop shop.
- Leave the flag in when you chip.

- Always use your favorite club to chip with, just one club, the one you're most comfortable with. By only chipping with only one club, you'll become better at judging distances and get your chip shots in closer.
- The higher the loft on the club you're chipping with, the more backspin will be created, so the ball will have less roll. The lower the loft on the clubface you're chipping with, the less backspin will be created, so the ball will have more roll.
- You need lots of imagination, creativity & visualization when you are chipping around the green.
- Don't forget to read the green the same as you would for a putt.
- Watch other people chip and watch their rolls to take tips for yourself.
- Chipping is all about judging distance, not direction. Chipping straight is guaranteed if you are aligned correctly and you should always be lined up correctly anyways. Lining up correctly is a given.
- Breathe in deep, then out fully, this is the trigger to start the swing. Don't breathe again until after contact with the ball. Holding your breath helps to create deathly silence and calm, perfect for both putting and chipping.
- Don't just chip to get on the green or to get close, aim to get every chip shot you make in the hole. Always aim for the bulls-eye.
- Visualize the chip shot you want to make before you chip the ball.
- Do practice swings while looking at the target, the landing area, the bull's eye. Try to visualize and practice how hard to make the swing. Get a good feeling for the distance.
- Choose a spot to land the ball on the green that is flat and gives you an even bounce, or aim for a dip because balls bounce in unpredictable directions off a hump. If the landing area is humpy, then you'll need to fly the ball in there with a flop shot.
- Aim for a specific landing area to land the ball, preferably on the green. Concentrate on that area and aim to hit the ball there. It's like a bull's-eye target. This visualization will help you focus on something distinct & positive, not anything else. Focusing on a specific spot you want to land on will significantly increase your chances of landing the ball there.

- Make sure you aim to leave yourself with level or uphill putts which are easier to make, not downhill or side hill putts which are harder to make.

Chipping From The Rough

- Chip shots from the rough have less backspin because it is harder to hit the ball cleanly. You will therefore have more roll on landing than from a regular chip shot off the fairway.
- If the rough is super deep, don't chip, you'll have to use a flop shot.

Flop Shots

- The ball will fly most of the way there & there won't be much roll.
- Most people tend to leave flop shots short. Don't be afraid. Be aggressive with flop shots. You can't go out-of-bounds, so don't be passive or worried. Go for it!
- When you are in between yardage and not sure what club to use for a flop shot, always go with the longer one. Club up, and swing easy.

(F-4) Greenside Sand Bunker Swing Routine

Key Points

- Don't forget to read the green the same as you would for a putt. You will generally need to swing approximately twice as hard as you would for a regular fairway shot from the same distance.
- Visualize the shot's ball flight.
- Concentrate on how much sand you will take, how deep you will go down & how long through the sand you will go.
- Most people leave splash bunker shots short. Don't be afraid, just go for it.

- The most important thing in the sand is to at least make sure you get out with just one stroke. Getting close to the target is your second priority. As the saying goes "if in doubt, just get out."

(F-5) Putting Swing Routine

How To Make The Perfect Putt
- Visualize how the ball is going to roll. Focus on the ball track you want the ball to roll on.
- Choose the distance & line of the putt you want to make at the exact same time.
- Keep everything square and let the putterhead flow back & forth trying to find the correct aimline. This will help you to understand how much true break there really is. Don't make any compensations, let the putter head flow back & forth as you figure out the true break.

Set Everything Up Parallel To Your Aimline
- Your shoulders are the most important to have set up perfectly parallel to your aimline.
- Your forearms are the second most important to have set up perfectly parallel to your aimline.
- Your eyes are the third most important to have set up perfectly parallel to your aimline.
- The rest are less important, but your hips, knees & feet also need to be perfectly parallel to your aimline.
- Judge the break to the center of the hole, not to the edge.

How Make The Perfect Putt
- Treat every putt as a straight putt. You don't cause the roll, the ground does. You just strike the ball out straight. Whatever curve the ball follows after that, just happens. It has nothing to do with how you rolled the ball because you always roll the ball out straight.

- Don't think about the speed of the ball in your mind's eye, think about the distance you want the ball to roll. You subconscious mind will automatically figure out the speed for you.
- Once you are on the green, remember that you're allowed to pick up the ball and place it back down lining up the writing or mark on the ball directly at the hole. This can help you to align up your whole putting stance more accurately by having a reference or guideline. It may also be a good time to clean your ball if it is dirty or muddy.

Walk Off The Distance

- Walk off the distance of your putts so you know the exact distance to the hole within a foot. Never guess the distance.

Make Your Putting Routine A Habit

- Don't spend too much time thinking about your putting routine or putting stroke as you prepare.
- You want to use the little bit of time you have focusing on the feel and touch of your putts for the perfect distance.
- Great putting comes out of habit, not out of planning it out every time.

Reading The Green

- Start observing the overall terrain and topographical features as you walk up towards the green.
- What is the slope? Is the ball going to be rolling uphill or downhill?
- How much will the putt break? Is the ball going to roll left-to-right or right-to-left?
- What is the distance from your ball to the hole?
- How strong is the wind? From what direction?
- How fast or slow is the green?

Preparing For A Putt

- Walk halfway to the hole and take a side view of the line to help determine slope.
- Stand about six feet behind the hole and look at your ball imagining the perfect ball track.
- Have a look to see where the downside of the hole is? If you were to pour water into the hole, which direction would the water flow out? Water always flows downhill.
- Step off the distance as you walk back to your ball. Feel the slope of the ground under your feet as you walk back as well. Take note in your mind of the distance.
- Crouch down about six feet behind the ball and look towards the hole concentrating on the perfect ball track line.
- Blink your eyes a couple times to re-adjust your vision.
- Cup your hands at the sides of your eyes to narrow your view and create tunnel vision looking up at the hole with your eyes horizontal to the ground. This helps you focus in. Imagine & visualize the perfect ball track rolling your ball right into the hole.
- Stand up while keeping your eyes focused on the line between the ball and hole.
- Don't pull your head back from the line, keep your eyes over the line as you get into your setup position.

Go With Your First Instinct

- Don't ever second guess yourself.
- Once you make a decision on the break & distance of your putt, lock it in.
- If you're still guessing or changing your mind by the time you're getting ready to putt, you'll almost always be wrong.
- More often than not, going with your first instinct is the correct decision.

The Putting Routine

- Take two steps back from the ball.
- Make the perfect grip while focusing on an imaginary target 18 inches past the hole.

- Visualize the perfect shot once again in your mind's eye. See it in your mind, watch it roll, watch it go all the way, a nice flowing putt, perfectly rolling to the imaginary target.
- Do a couple practice swings concentrating on feeling distance is the only thing on your mind. Visualize yourself swinging to hit the ball that exact distance.

Pre-Shot Routine

- Walk back into your stance and line yourself up on your aimline with a perfectly square putterface and perfectly square body. Make sure you are lined up 100% parallel to your aimline.
- Consciously stand up as tall & erect as you can & tighten your abdominal muscles.
- Waggle your hands, knees, arms and shoulders to get loose for the swing. Release all tension.
- Take in one last deep breath and breathe out all air. Hold your breath & relax for the rest of the swing. There is a deathly silence & calm for the rest of the swing.

The Putting Ritual

- Lift the putterhead a touch off the ground, then place it back down by tapping the ground. This is the trigger to the brain that the ritual has begun & there is no turning back.
- Take one last look down your aimline to the imaginary target 18 inches past the hole.
- Look back down at the ball with your eyes perfectly parallel to the aimline.
- Take the putterhead back as gently as you can in the smoothest takeaway you can make it.
- Concentrate on rolling the ball the perfect distance is the only thing on your mind now.
- Hold the putter at the top of the followthrough for three seconds & start breathing normally again.
- Walk out of your stance & into the future slowly & peacefully.

(G)
Managing Your Game

(G-1) Mental Reminders

Warm Up
- Start off with some stretches to warm up your muscles and to loosen them up.
- Take lots of deep breaths. This will help to calm your nerves.
- You need soft muscles before you start a game because soft muscles work smoother than tight muscles.
- The warm-up is all about finding your rhythm & getting in the grove, not to work on or change your swing mechanics. Working on and changing your swing mechanics is for practice sessions only.

Get In The Zone
- Block everything out of your mind, except for the pure focus on what you're trying to accomplish.
- Don't ever let anything break your concentration and if something or someone does, simply re-group & press on.
- Decide that nothing is going to bother you for 18 holes, nothing! Not the weather, not another player, not even a bad shot or a bad score.
- Don't clutter your mind with thoughts that you know shouldn't be there.
- Love competition & love pressure. This is part of the enjoyment, this is the rush.
- You need to get yourself in the zone before each & every game, before each & every shot.
- Be your own biggest cheerleader. Cheer yourself on!

Concentrate

- Pay attention to detail.
- Always take the game serious.
- Always concentrate & focus on making the best shot for each & every shot you take.
- Play your best game and let your opponent play theirs. That's all you can do.

Control & Discipline

- Make sure you take the initiative to control your mind and to control what it thinks about around the course.
- Control your emotions & don't let outside stuff get to you.
- Form yourself very careful & simple to follow habits.
- Follow a rigid & well programmed plan of attack for 18 holes straight.
- You'll need tremendous discipline in order to be successful on a golf course.

Determination

- Have a passion & dig deep from your heart for every single shot you take.
- Put everything you got into every single shot.
- Always try your best. Never get lazy.
- You need a fierce, intense & competitive streak within you.
- Get excited & get pumped up!
- Be relentless!
- Persevere. Always hang in there.
- Never give up! Only try harder in the face of adversity.
- Run past the finish line, never to it.

Stay In The Present Moment

- Simply aim to make every shot your best shot.
- Always ignore the past and future. Don't anticipate the future or worry about what has happened in the past.
- Stay in the present at all times. Live in the moment. Never get ahead or behind yourself.

- Learn to forget very quickly about what went wrong in the past. Ignore all disasters & catastrophes, they happen to everyone, not just you.
- Never get anxious about future shots either.
- You are only ever thinking 100% of the time about one shot only, the current shot you are about to take.
- Learn to immediately step out of the past and into the present after each and every shot.
- Stay in the present moment. It will make golf much more enjoyable & improve your score too.

Don't Count Your Score

- Never add up your score as you play and never strive for a certain score either. Add it all up at the end of the game.
- Just play a bunch of small games. Don't think of the whole round as one big game. Make each shot its own little game within itself.
- Try to make each shot the best shot possible, the best shot you can make it and see how many good shots you can make in a round.
- Don't have any expectations for the day. Never worry about what the outcome is going to be. You are only as good as you are, let it be. There is always good score days and bad score days. Whatever is going to happen is just going to happen. All you can do is try your best.

In Between Shots

- Laugh, joke, relax, enjoy the view, enjoy the course, enjoy your company, be happy, positive & have fun! That's what you're there for.
- There is lots of time in between shots to think about what has just happened and what you want to happen in the future, but don't think about it. Stay in the present moment.
- Do everything in slow motion, never rush anywhere or rush anything that you're doing.

Positive Thinking Only

- Have positive thoughts 100% of the time, it'll enhance your performance.
- Negative thoughts are never allowed.
- Fight off all negative energy.
- Have a positive outlook & be optimistic.
- Having a bad attitude is no fun at all & will only end up ruining your score.

Confidence

- Trust & believe in yourself.
- Have a no fear attitude.
- Have lots of confidence as it will most definitely increase your chances of hitting a good shot.
- It's normal to be nervous & have some anxiety, but never be intimidated or afraid.
- You need all the confidence in the world, but be careful not to develop an ego. Nobody likes to play golf with a person with an ego. That is just not fun at all.
- Be humble about all your good shots & all your good rounds.

Decisive Decisions Only

- Your decisions need to be decisive, confident & not half guessing.
- You need control of your mind.
- Don't be overly analytical on the course, let your instincts take over & make quick & distinct decisions only.

(G-2) Emotional Control

Have Fun!

- Don't forget to smell the roses along the way.
- It's just a game. Games are meant to be fun.
- Laugh lots. Smile lots. Joke lots.
- Enjoy your day better than you enjoy the golf.
- Appreciate the course and people you are with.

- Golf is more about the people you play with than the score you shoot.
- Be friendly, have good manners and follow proper golf etiquette.
- A bad round of golf is better than a good day at work.
- Just be happy.

Slow Down

- Take your time.
- Don't rush through anything you do during the day.
- Relax and enjoy life & the friends you are with.
- Be comfortable.
- Be laid back & easygoing.
- Calm thoughts only.
- Always play golf slowly & patiently.

Go With The Flow

- Take off your watch & forget about the time.
- Feel as loose and carefree as the wind is on the course. The more relaxed and easygoing you are, the more freely you'll swing your clubs.
- Never blame the course or conditions, don't even blame yourself. What has just happened, just happened and was meant to be.
- Realize that golf is very similar to the stock market. How it performs at any given moment is not a true representation of the stock. It goes through daily ups and downs and lengthy bust and boom cycles just like you do as a golf player.
- Be laid back, it'll improve your score.

Don't Be Worried

- Worrying too much will lead to thinking too much. Thinking too much will lead to taking too much time & slowing down the game. You'll be frustrating the people on the course with you and disrupting your own natural flow & rhythm. Being worried will ultimately ruin your score.
- Always feel at ease & never be afraid of hitting a bad shot. Think positively.

- Feel as loose and as carefree as you can all day long.

Neutral Emotions

- Keep your emotions under control.
- Always stay on neutral emotions, neither up nor down, indifferent. You are not happy, you are not angry, you are neutral.
- Treat good golf shots & bad golf shots the same way. They're just another golf shot. It's just another day.

Anger & Failure Management

- Getting angry or frustrated will only poison your soul & poisoning your soul will definitely not help you make better golf shots.
- Remember that a poor golf shot is always just a swing away, so don't be so surprised when it happens. Be prepared, anticipate & accept all your poor golf shots before they even happen.
- Accept the fact that it is impossible to make a perfect shot every single time. When you hit a poor shot, just laugh about it.
- How you handle your poor golf shots is much more of a concern to you than how you handle your good golf shots. Don't get angry!

Short Bursts Of Emotions

- It's ok to have a short burst of emotion for a few seconds.
- A burst of anger or excitement or disappointment is totally natural & ok, but get back to your neutral emotions right away. Not as soon as possible, but right away! (within 3-10 seconds)

Handling Disasters / Catastrophes

- Never get overwhelmed and lose control by any situation, no matter how bad it is or gets.
- Keep your composure & always remain calm. Just move on.
- You can't always control what happens to you, but you can control how you react to what's happened to you.

- After a disaster or catastrophe, smile & laugh. It is the most beneficial thing you can do.
- Learn to look adversity straight in the face with a great big smile.

(G-3) Planning Shots

Game Day Planning

- Everything that happens on the course needs to be automatic. You should be thinking, but you should not be thinking about what to think about.
- Establish your game plan before you get to the course, not during it.
- Use the golf course map to help you plan your shots.
- The simpler & more organized your plan, the more fun you'll have & the lower your score will be.
- Get to the course at least 30 minutes early to give yourself time to relax, warm-up & clear your mind.
- Your thoughts need to have a routine & flow in the right direction.
- Keep your thought processes the exact same every single time. It will become habit, second nature, routine & you will become a more consistent golfer because of it.

Always Play The Safest Most Probable Shot

- Avoid taking risks and put your mind at ease. Only play safe shots.
- Always aim away from trouble.

Tee Shots

- The very first tee shot always gives people the jitters, especially if spectators are there watching. Your only priority is to get the ball down the center of the fairway and safe in play, don't worry so much about distance.
- Just relax & make an easy & smooth swing.

- Use a club you're most comfortable with, it doesn't always have to be the driver.
- Getting the ball out there safely sets your mind up for confidence & gets you off on the right start & in control of your game.

Short Distances

- Play all your short shots aggressively to the green or to the flag. There is no need to play a short shot safe unless obvious danger is near.
- Don't be passive or tentative on your short shots, go for it!
- You don't always need to aim for the flag either. You should sometimes just aim for the dead center of the green giving you a larger cushion for margin of error. Just getting on the green is so important.

Long Distances

- Play all your long shots safely.
- Be extra careful.
- Keeping the shot straight is your number one priority.
- Just get it out there. Never press for distance. Keep the ball straight!

Type Of Ball To Use

- Always use the same ball. Never mix different brands or types. Get used to just one type of ball.

Swing Strategies

- Driver: Straight is the priority. (not distance)
- Fairway Woods: Straight is the priority. (not distance)
- Long / Middle Irons: Straight is the priority. (not distance)
- Short Irons - Pitching: *** Straight is the priority & distance control is the priority equally. *** These shots are a very big challenge to be dropped in close. You need to be next to perfect at these shots. Practice these shots the most.
- Chipping: Distance is the priority. (not straight)

- <u>Long / Medium Putts</u>: Distance is the priority. (not straight)
- <u>Short Putts</u>: Straight is the priority. (not distance)

Placing Shots

- Always notice where it is best to miss your shot. Long, short, left or right?
- Start thinking where you want to take your next shot from. You want to leave yourself with the best angle & distance to the flag.
- Know the pin placement.
- Know the slope and size of the green.
- Know what bunkers or water is around the green so you can stay away from trouble.
- Know your favorite shots and favorite distances & try to hit the ball there. Example: If your favorite distance is a full 100 yard shot with a 9-iron & the hole is 320 yards long, then hit a 5-iron 220 yards. There would be no need to drive the ball off the tee then.
- Often laying up on a shot is your best shot.

Shake Your Body

- Shake your legs, arms & hands whenever you want to, whenever you need to, in order to stay loose. It also helps to get rid of any tension and nervousness.

Visualizing & Imagination

- You need to have great imagination and be able to visualize your shots through the air and visualize yourself making the perfect rhythmic swing before you actually make them.
- Keep visualizing all your shots and never stop.

When Taking A Shot

- You can't have any doubts when you're standing over the ball ready to make a swing. Having doubt & being undecided will result in a nervous & tentative swing that will usually conclude with a mishit.

- Don't be defensive. Raise your expectations, expect to hit a great shot.
- Focus & zone in with positive and confident thoughts only.
- Concentrate on feeling your hands for the entire swing, it helps to keep the swing smooth & rhythmic.

(G-4) The Weather

Windy Days

- Draw a big arrow on the scorecard map for reference on which general direction the wind is blowing.
- Look up in the sky to see which way the clouds are moving and how fast.
- Look at the tree tops to see which way the trees are swaying.
- Check a flag at another hole to see how fast and what direction the flag is blowing.
- Pick up some blades of grass and throw them to see what direction and how fast they blow.
- Keep the ball low. Punching the ball low is the best strategy on windy days.
- Move the ball farther back in your stance to help keep the ball low.
- Tee the ball slightly lower than normal will reduce under spin on the ball & keep the ball from climbing up into the air.
- Use more of a sweeping blow than a descending blow for all your swings to keep the ball low.
- Lower your hands in the followthrough will help to keep the ball low.
- Widen your stance more than normal to help keep the ball low & to help keep your balance in the blowing wind.

Headwind

- Temptation is to swing harder into the wind, but don't.
- Take more club and swing easier. As the saying goes "swing with ease in to the breeze". This reduces backspin and stops the ball from climbing up into the air.

- Hitting a ball into the wind increases the spinning on the ball in all directions. Therefore, controlling the ball will be more effective. In other words, it will be easier to fade or draw the ball into a headwind. But, it will also be easier to lose control and hook or slice your shot too. Therefore, you need to be extra careful into a headwind.
- The ball will not travel as far as normal and will have more backspin.
- The ball will not roll as much on landing.

Tailwind

- Hitting a ball with the wind decreases the spinning on the ball in all directions. Therefore, controlling the ball will be less effective. In other words, it will be harder to fade or draw the ball with the wind. But, it will also be harder to lose control and hook or slice your shot too. Therefore, you don't need to be as careful into a tailwind.
- The ball will travel farther than normal and will have less backspin.
- The ball will roll more on landing.

Crosswind

- You can either shape your shot with a fade or draw, or you can adjust your aim to account for the crosswind.
- The stronger the crosswind, the more you'll need to adjust.

Hot Days

- Greens tend to be faster.
- Hot balls fly farther than cold balls. Your distances will be farther.
- Sand traps will be lighter & fluffier.

Cold Days

- Greens tend to be slower.
- Cold balls fly shorter than hot balls. Your distances will be less.

- Sand traps will be heavier & dense.

Rainy & Wet Days
- Soaking wet greens will be softer, slower and the ball will stop quickly.
- Slightly wet greens will be softer & slower too, but the greens are slippery and ball will skid on landing.
- Hitting out of wet grass reduces backspin on the ball, so your ball will roll more.
- A wet ball tends to dive rather than fly. Therefore, always dry your ball off before you tee it up.

(G-5) Swinging The Club

Swinging Too Hard
- If you swing too hard, you will almost always mishit the shot you are trying to make. So, never swing too hard. Always swing at 85% of maximum power at the most.
- Keep your swinging tempo & rhythm under control at all times.
- Swing easy and just accept the fact that the ball will not always be able to fly as far as you'd like it to.

Rhythm
- Smoothness & rhythm begins in your mind and heart.
- Having perfect rhythm & smoothness to your swing is the number one priority on the golf course.
- Don't try to control the rhythm. Follow it, flow with it.
- Allow your clubhead to lead throughout the entire swing.
- Concentrate on feeling your hands and the clubhead throughout the entire swing.
- A slower backswing leads to better rhythm. (within reason)
- A golf swing is like a ballet dance.
- Never tighten your muscles and try to strike the ball. Your muscles need to be as loose & comfortable as can be.
- A perfectly timed swing is effortless.

- When a club is swung properly you are not conscious of what is happening in all the mechanics of the swing. The only thing you feel is your hands & the clubhead swinging around you.
- Rhythm is like swinging on a swing set. Once swung back it reaches a natural stopping point and starts down again on its own natural momentum.
- Swing at the same rhythm for every shot you make no matter how short or long the swing is. Also, swing at the same rhythm for every single club no matter if it is the driver or a wedge.
- The lighter you can grip a club, the better your rhythm will be.
- Don't ever try to steer the clubhead, it needs to be freewheeling with the freedom to flow. The freedom of a swing is almost careless like.
- Patience is key to having good rhythm.
- Having a good constant & repeatable rhythm will help you swing better. It will also make you more confident and help to eliminate thinking.
- Find your very own personal rhythm and never change it. Some people have faster or slower rhythm's than others. Your rhythm is unique to yourself. Swing at a rhythm consistent with the way you naturally move your body.

Smoothness
- Never try to hit the ball, swing through the ball that just happens to get in the way.
- Keep all your muscles loose and stretched.
- Make sure you always have more than enough club & swing easy.
- A swing is loosening of the muscles, whereas a hit is tightening of the muscles. Golfing is a swing, not a hit. When you hit a ball like in baseball, you tighten all your muscles.
- Think round, circle, smooth, slow, lazy, easy, natural, not too quickly, beautifully, harmonious, artistic, balanced, relaxed, graceful, consistent, effortlessly, under control.
- A good swing has a distinct and gratifying feel to it.

Touch

- Touch is the ability to know the exact amount to accelerate for the perfect distance.
- Touch is knowing how long a shot is and how much power it will require.
- Add a little bit of extra touch to every shot you make.

Tempo / Speed

- You cannot interrupt the natural motion of a golf swing. In other words, you can't accelerate it or slow it down in the middle of your swing, it needs to flow naturally.
- Find the natural tempo & speed of your swing that suits your personality. Some people naturally swing fast, some people naturally swing slow and some people are in between. Everyone's speed & tempo is different & unique to the individual.

Feel

- You know how far back in your backswing you want to go and you know how far you want the ball to go and 'feel' is the ability to feel that distance in your swing.
- During practice swings ask yourself "How does this swing feel?" A little more or a little less or is it just right? This is feel.
- You need to figure out what feels right for the perfect swing you have imagined in your mind.
- Feel is knowing how much power to apply, how to get your ball there.

(G-6) Distance Of Clubs

Key Points

- You need to know exactly how far every single one of your club's will go.
- Keep track & re-check your personal distances every once in a while because they can change over time.

- The higher you hit the ball, the less you need to worry about distance and the more you need to worry about keeping it straight.
- The lower you hit the ball, such as a bump-and-run or chip shot, the less you need to worry about keeping it straight and the more you need to worry about distance.
- Bring out a chart with all your distances, heights & rolls recorded. This way you don't have to guess on the course, you can easily & quickly check. Take away all the guess work and all your shots will be much more accurate. Your confidence will be much higher as well because you will know exactly what shot you need to take each & every time.

The Clock (O'Clock)

- This is how you measure all your swings for distance.
- How far back you take your left arm is the hour hand on the clock. (Note: The clubshaft is never the hour hand, your left arm is always the hour hand)
- At address your left arm is at 6 O'clock. Take the clubhead back a little so your hand is over your back right knee is 7 O'clock. A little more is 8 O'clock. When your left arm is back parallel to the ground is 9 O'clock. A little more is 10 O'clock. A full fullswing into the perfect box structure is 11 O'clock.
- You can even break the difference and name your shots 8:30 or 9:30 or 10:30 to be a little more precise.
- This is how you reference your distances for each club you have.

Roll Of Each Club

- It's also good to note how much each of your shots will roll.

Trajectory Of Each Club

- It's also good to note how high each of your shots will go. You don't want to get caught up in the tree branches.

Reducing Distance

- There is another simple way to reduce the distance for each club. It's to grip down on the club, move a little closer to the ball & make the same swing.

Calculating Distances

- Most distances on a course are measured from the middle of the fairway to the middle of the green. Therefore, you'll need to add or subtract distance when you are off to the side of the fairway shooting on an angle.
- Check the flag position. Is it in the front or back of the green? You will need to add or subtract distance accordingly.
- Are you hitting the ball uphill, downhill or flat? You will need to add, subtract or keep the distance the same.

Backspin

- All golf shots are descending blows with some degree of backspin with the exception of the driver which is a sweeping level off a tee.
- Backspin helps the ball fly through the air more accurately. The more backspin, the straighter the ball will fly & less the ball will roll.

Example Of Distance Charts

Pitching Wedge

10 yards = 7 O'clock
20 yards = 8 O'clock
30 yards = 9 O'clock
40 yards = 9:30
50 yards = 10 O'clock
60 yards = 10:30

(Where the ball lands, not where the ball rolls to)

The Full Power Swing

45 yards = PW (grip down)
55 yards = PW
90 yards = 9-Iron (grip down)
100 yards = 9-Iron
110 yards = 8-Iron (grip down)
120 yards = 8-Iron
130 yards = 7-Iron (grip down)
140 yards = 7-Iron
150 yards = 6-Iron (grip down)
160 yards = 6-Iron
170 yards = 5-Iron (grip down)
180 yards = 5-Iron
190 yards = 4-Iron (grip down)
200 yards = 4-Iron
210 yards = 3-Iron (grip down)
220 yards = 3-Iron
230 yards = 5-wood (grip down)

240 yards = 5-wood

250 yards = 3-wood (grip down)

260 yards = 3-wood

270 yards = Driver (grip down)

280 yards = Driver

(This is where the ball ends up, its final location after the total flight and roll)

Chipping & Rolls (Pitching Wedge)

7 O'clock = 30 feet with a 10 foot roll = 40 feet

8 O'clock = 50 feet with a 20 foot roll = 70 feet

9 O'clock = 60 feet with a 30 foot roll = 90 feet

10 O'clock = 70 feet with a 40 foot roll = 110 feet

(G-7) Practicing To Get Better

Key Points

- You are only as good as your weakest link. Find your weakest link and improve on it.
- Take the complexity of a golf swing and break it down into the simple.
- Be as specific as you can. Focus on one thing at a time. Don't try to improve everything at the same time.
- Practice the same way that you play by treating each shot very carefully. It's slower and it takes more effort & time for each shot, but you'll improve faster.
- Make sure you practice lots. The driving range is a perfect place to work on your game and improve your golf score for the future which in turn makes golf even more fun.
- Practicing is the key to getting better, not just playing rounds.
- Find ways to love practicing so it's not so boring and doesn't seem like work.

- Treat every practice shot as if it is as important as a real shot in a game.
- Don't rush through your practice sessions, have patience or you'll be in danger of making your swing worse.
- Work harder at the practice range than you do on the golf course.
- Use your practice time effectively. You need discipline and a procedure to follow, a plan.

Practicing Is Fun!

- Golf should never be boring even when you're practicing. So do everything you can to enjoy yourself and have fun even when practicing too.
- You'll learn faster if you're always challenging yourself and having fun.
- Have competitions with yourself when practicing. As often as possible compete against yourself & if possible someone else. You'll sharpen your skills faster, time will go faster & you'll have more fun.
- Practicing does not need to be tedious. Take your time.

Simpler Is Better

- The simpler your swing is, the easier it will be to learn and repeat & the easier it will be to execute with precision and accuracy as well.
- Don't make your swing any more complicated than it needs to be.
- Simplicity is repeatable, reliable, consistent & able to hold up under pressure.
- KISS – Keep it simple stupid. You need to keep everything as simple as possible.

Use Learning Aids

- It's a great idea to use a lot of different learning aids when practicing. There are a bunch out there. Many home made & simple and many are store bought & more complex.

- Example: Use two clubs and line them up parallel to your aimline to form railroad tracks. One along your feet and one just outside the ball. Make sure you have a spot mark out in front of your ball and practice this way. Railroad tracks make sure that you are lined up to your target correctly & that your feet, hips, shoulders & eyes are all lined up correctly as well. This is the simplest and most important learning aid that there is.
- Never hit a practice shot with bad alignment. Use railroad tracks a lot of the time no matter how good you get. This will always keep your alignment in check.
- Practice your precise yardage. That is why the yardage signs are there. Don't just practice direction. How far are your shots going?
- Aim at multiple targets when you practice, not always the same one. Use as many different targets as possible. Mix it up.

What To Practice

- Constantly find the newest discovered weakest link in your golf game and improve on it.
- The more specific you can be, the better. You are only as good as your weakest link.
- Think of your golf swing as an efficient running machine. Each part is dependent on the other running parts. So if one part is not functioning properly, the other parts are going to be affected. Don't have any broken parts in your machine.
- Spend almost all of your time practicing your weakest areas.
- Spend quite a bit of time working and practicing on your mediocre areas.
- Spend a little bit of time refining and working on your strongest areas.
- Most of your shots on the golf course will be the ones 100 yards or less, so practice these shots the most. (pitching, chipping & putting)
- The short game is where the money is at. In other words, this is where you need to get real good if you want to significantly lower your score.

Perfect Practice Makes Perfect

- Practicing is all about quality not quantity.
- It's not about how many balls you hit or how long your practiced. It's all about how you spend your time when you do practice.
- The saying you often hear is that "practice makes perfect" and that is very wrong! What you should be hearing is that "perfect practice makes perfect" because this is very correct.
- Practice doesn't make perfect. Practice makes permanent. So be careful how you practice. Practice correctly or don't even practice at all, because only perfect practice makes perfect!
- Practice properly, correctly, patiently, slowly & perfectly. That's the only way to practice.
- Never practice carelessly & quickly just firing off shots & beating away at balls. That's just ridiculous!
- Perfect repetitions lead to the formation of near perfect habits that lead to near perfect swings on the golf course.
- The more you practice perfectly, the faster you'll improve.
- Only perfect practice helps you move towards perfection.
- If you really don't feel in the mood to practice one day, then don't. Do yourself a massive favor.
- If you really must practice when you don't feel like it, at least shorten the time, hit less balls & try to work smarter, not harder.
- Always remember & never forget that "perfect practice makes perfect" not just practicing.

How To Form A Habit

- Treat each shot at the driving range as a real shot in a real game situation.
- You need to do the exact same thing 10,000 times in a row to make it a habit. (20,000 times to have in ingrained permanently) Therefore, practice doing the exact same correct swing in the exact same manner for your next 10,000 swings. If you are swinging differently all the time, you will never form a habit.
- No practice is always a better than bad practice. Grooving bad swings will ensure poor swing habits over the long-term. You'll not only be wasting your time, you'll be making your swing worse.

- Poor practice ingrains poor habits. Therefore, do your best to practice correctly because perfect practice is what ingrains good habits & good habits is what creates good golfers.

Exercise
- You need to be in good shape in order to play good golf.
- The better shape you are in, the better you will be able to hold everything up in proper posture and endure the long round of golf in the hot sun.
- Make sure you are fully hydrated with water before and during the round.
- Always eat healthy before & during the round.
- Both your cardiovascular shape & physical muscular strength are very important.

Keep Learning Forever
- Never stop learning and improving. Keep reading books, keep playing and keep practicing.
- Most importantly, have fun!
- All the best of luck to you!

(H)
Bibliography

(H-1) References Used To
Help Write This Book

- Adams, Mike, *The Complete Golf Manual*, Carlton Books, 2001.

- Cambell, Malcom, *Ultimate Golf Techniques*, Firefly Books, 1998.

- Canfield, Jack, *Chicken Soup for the Golfer's Soul*, Health Communictions, 1998.

- Cohn, Patrick J. *The Mental Art of Putting*, Taylor Trade Publishing, 1995.

- Harmon, Butch, *Butch Harmon's Playing Lessons*, Fireside, 1999.

- Leadbetter, *David, 100% Golf – How to Unlock Your True Golfing Potential*, Harper Collins Publishers, 2002.

- Mastroni, Nick, *Master Strokes*, Running Press, 2003.

- McCord, Robert, *The Best Advice Ever For Golfers*, Andrew McMeel Publishing, 2001.

- Minni, Scott, *Smash & Carve Golf*, Canadian Cataloguing in Publication Data, 1999.

- Montgomerie, Colin, *K-I-S-S Guide to Playing Golf*, Dorling Kindersley, 2000.

- Newell, Steve, *The Golf Instruction Manual*, Dorling Kindersley, 2001.

- Pelz, Dave, *Dave Pelz's Putting Bible*, DoubleDay, 2000.

- Pelz, Dave, *Dave Pelz's Short Game Bible*, Double Day, 2000.

- Sole, Mel, *Golf Step-by-Step*, PRC Publishing, 2002.

- Toski, Bob, *How to Feel a Real Golf Swing*, Three Rivers Press, 1997.

- United States Golf Teachers Federation, *Driving Tips*, Remy Media, 2002.

- United States Golf Teachers Federation, *Putting Tips*, Remy Media, 2002.

- United States Golf Teachers Federation, *Short Game Tips*, Remy Media, 2002.

- Voorhees, Randy, *The Little Book of Golf Slang*, Andrews McMeel Publishing, 1997.

- Weir, Mike, *On Course with Mike Wier*, McGraw-Hill Ryerson, 2001.

- Wood, Mark, *Master Golf*, Sterling Publishig, 2002.

- Woods, Tiger, *Tiger Woods How I Play Golf*, Warner Books, 2001.

- Wright, Nick, *The Best Golf Tips Ever*, Thomas Allen Publishers, 2003.

- Zumerchik, John, *Newton On the Tee,* Simon & Schuster, 2002.